FOR USE
IN
LIBRARY
ONLY

D1228565

THOMAS MIDDLETON

GARLAND REFERENCE LIBRARY
OF THE HUMANITIES
(VOL. 554)

THOMAS MIDDLETON
An Annotated Bibliography

Dorothy Wolff

GARLAND PUBLISHING INC. • NEW YORK & LONDON
1985

Library of Congress Cataloging in Publication Data

Wolff, Dorothy, 1954–
Thomas Middleton : an annotated bibliography.

(Garland reference library of the humanities ; vol. 554)
Includes index.
1. Middleton, Thomas, d. 1627—Bibliography.
I. Title. II. Series: Garland reference library of the humanities ; v. 554.
Z8574.W64 1985 [PR2716] 016.822′3 84-45367
ISBN 0-8240-8819-0 (alk. paper)

Printed on acid-free, 250-year-life paper
Manufactured in the United States of America

CONTENTS

INTRODUCTION

Thomas Middleton has long been the focus of critical attention and controversy. He has been called a detached observer of Jacobean London life, a cynical opportunist playing on his audience's appetite for vice and crime, a realist or naturalist with sympathy for human weakness, a genial writer on the human condition, a satirist with or without moral viewpoint, a playwright torn between his interest in the grotesque and his moral values, and a stern Puritan moralist. During the past century, his plays, prose, and poetry have been the subjects of considerable critical attention. This annotated bibliography is meant to be a guide, both for the casual undergraduate student and the more serious researcher, to what is generally available in the field of Middleton research and to which critical works are most useful in general and specific areas. The citations, with one or two exceptions, are post-1900; for a reasonably complete pre-1900 listing, see Tannenbaum's *Elizabethan Bibliographies*, listed in Part Five.

The bibliography is divided into sections according to the type of material listed. In the first section are included all monographs. The first part of this section consists of general monograph studies in the Jacobean drama. This part is not exhaustive in scope; it contains primarily those works which have either made a permanent mark on literary criticism or are in some way of special interest to Middleton students or critics because they contain sizeable references to or chapters on Middleton or provide important background material to his works.

In the second part of this section are listed monographs concerned chiefly or entirely with Middleton's work. This part is comprehensive, although I have not included thesis or dissertation manuscripts --where these have merited extensive consideration, they have generally in due course received publication in one form or another and so are duly listed; those still in manuscript can easily be found in abstract form.

In the second section are those periodical or collected articles which refer directly to Middleton's life or work, or contain passing references to his work. This section is also comprehensive; general students may find this area of most use, as the bulk of Middleton criticism exists in essay and article form.

The third section is a list of primary materials available in modern editions, or in the case of works for which no modern edition has yet been prepared, the best facsimile edition or the most recent "standard" edition available, or both. I have made no effort to track down manuscript or microfilm texts; the former are out of the scope of this work and the latter are available to any student with a *Short Title Catalogue*. Collections of plays published this century and containing plays by Middleton are listed in the first part of this section, alphabetically by editor or general editor.

I have included references to plays of disputed authorship, including such perennial favourites as *The Revenger's Tragedy* and the Hecate scenes of *Macbeth*. (A list of plays considered part or possibility part of the Middleton canon appears in the Appendix.) These references are by and large concerned with authorship; I have not included all general critical references to plays that are on occasion attributed to Middleton, if such references make no such attribution. Thus, for example, while most references to *The Second Maiden's Tragedy* are included because of the involvement of Middleton's name, any work on *A Yorkshire Tragedy*, to name only one play, that does not involve attribution studies concerning Middleton has not been considered within the scope of this bibliography.

The Revenger's Tragedy is a special case. At any one period, the bulk of criticism on this play has considered the authorship question as well as the play itself. To include every reference to the play would produce what would be in effect an annotated bibliography of Cyril Tourneur as well as Thomas Middleton; that is obviously beyond the scope of this bibliography. To give a fair view of Middleton's involvement with this play, and at the same time not to trespass on the territory of Tourneur bibliographers, I have included those articles on the play that are considered to be seminal, interesting, or provocative, both on authorship and on other considerations, and those items accepting Middleton as author (an increasing number) but otherwise not addressing the question. I refer the general *Revenger's Tragedy* student to the Tourneur bibliographies by Forker and Tucker listed in Part Five for comprehensive listings of "Tourneur" research and discussion, and for modern editions of *The Revenger's Tragedy* (see item 619).

The fourth section of the bibliography is a listing of those articles about Middleton which have appeared in languages other than English. Because some of these articles have been published in periodicals or languages not accessible to me, not all of the articles in this section have been read; I have, however, included comments whenever such information is available and have indicated the source of the listing when I have been unable to locate the article itself.

The final section is a bibliography of bibliographies. This section includes the major older secondary compilations, and more recent Jacobean or seventeenth-century listings which include Middleton. The present work is meant to incorporate the listings and complement the annotations of these bibliographies (except for the annual ones); with the exception of some general studies and the majority of nineteenth-century listings, this bibliography includes all previous ones. Listings later than the summer of 1983, with a few exceptions, have not been included; the bibliography is complete as of Winter 1983.

The annotations are designed to be of use to the researcher and student; they are therefore descriptive and evaluative. They are meant to provide a guide to the central point or approach of an article or monograph, a taste of its style or presentation, and, when appropriate, an estimation of its general or specific usefulness. Items which respond to, or are reacted to, by other items are cross-referenced, as are articles which, while not directly connected, do give opposite or alternate readings or interpretations of specific matters.

All items listed have been seen and read, with exception of those items found in Part Four (as explained above) and of a few items in the rest of the bibliography which I have been unable to view; these last are marked with [**] and are followed by a reference to the listing in which each was found (the full form of these references will be found in Part Five). I have annotated more extensively those items that I have found either helpful or misleading in my own research, but all evaluative comments reflect general critical reaction. I have included a selection of reviews; each has been included immediately following the listing of the work upon which it comments.

The appendix is a guide to the plays considered, by some or many, to form part of the Middleotn canon. I have indicated the most generally accepted date and authorship for each, with alternate attributions included as well. The appendix is meant to be complementary to the index, which lists citations by play.

I would like to express my thanks to Dr. A.S.G. Edwards of the University of Victoria, who first involved me in this project, and to my editors at Garland Publishing, Pamela Chergotis and Rita Quintas, who have been very understanding as a short-term project became a longer one. I would like to thank, first of all, Trevor Alexander, for his generosity with computer time, and my brother Michael Wolff and his assistants John Eaton and Robin Marrion for their invaluable proofreading and organisational help. I also thank Ming Jung for her time and help, and Maggie Pugh and Rudy van der Ham, without whose technical knowledge and kind assistance this bibliography could never have been completed.

ABBREVIATIONS

The following abbreviations appear throughout the work:

1. *Play Series* (these play series are published as follows):

   The Fountainwell Drama Texts: Oliver and Boyd, Edinburgh

   The New Mermaids: Ernest Benn, London

   Plays by Renaissance and Restoration Dramatists: Cambridge University Press, Cambridge

   Regent's Renaissance Drama Series: University of Nebraska, Lincoln (all cited plays in this series have a Middleton chronology)

   The Revels Plays: Methuen, London, and Manchester University Press, Manchester

   Studies in English Drama: Edward Arnold, London

2. *Periodical Titles*:

(n.s.)	new series
(o.s.)	old series
EIC	Essays in Criticism
ELN	English Language Notes
ELR	English Literary Renaissance
ESA	English Studies in Africa
E&S	Essay and Studies for the English Association
JEGP	Journal of English and German Philology
MLN	Modern Language Notes
MLQ	Modern Language Quarterly
MLR	Modern Language Review
MP	Modern Philology

NQ	Notes and Queries
PBSA	Publications of the Bibliographical Society of America
PLL	Papers on Language and Literature
PMLA	Publications of the Modern Language Society of America
PQ	Philological Quarterly
RenD	Renaissance Drama
RenP	Renaissance Papers
RES	Review of English Studies
SAB	Shakespeare Association Bulletin
SCN	Seventeenth Century News
SEL	Studies in English Literature
SP	Studies in Philology
SQ	Shakespeare Quarterly
TLS	Times Literary Supplement (London)
YES	The Yearbook of English Studies

3. *Collections*:

"Accompaninge the players"

"Accompaninge the players": Essays Celebrating Thomas Middleton, 1580-1980, ed. Kenneth Friedenreich. New York: AMS Press, 1983 (AMS Studies in the Renaissance 8). For a discussion of this collection, see item 142.

Elizabethan Drama

Elizabethan Drama: Modern Essays in Criticism, ed. R.J. Kaufman. New York: Oxford University Press, 1961.

Holzknecht

Studies in the English Renaissance Drama in Memory of Karl Julius Holzknecht, ed. J.W. Bennet, Oscar Cargill, and Vernon Hall, Jr. New York: New York University Press, 1959.

Joseph Quincy Adams Memorial Studies

Joseph Quincy Adams Memorial Studies, ed. James G. McManaway, Giles E. Dawson and Edwin E. Willoughby. Washington, D.C.: The Folger Shakespeare Library, 1948.

Shakespeare's Contemporaries

Shakespeare's Contemporaries: Modern Studies in English Renaissance Drama, ed. Max Bluestone and Norman Rabkin, with an introduction by Alfred Harbage. Englewood Cliffs, New Jersey: Prentice-Hall, 1970 (second edition; first edition 1961).

4. *Series of Critical Works*:

Salzburg *Salzburg Studies in English Literature* under the direction of Professor Erwin A. Sturzl. Salzburg, Austria: Institut für Anglistik und Amerikanistik, Universität Salzburg.

The publication documentation for all monographs and collections in this series is given as simply "Salzburg," with the date.

A NOTE ON SPELLING AND FORMAT

Article and book titles are given as published, with some normalisation of capitalisation in book subtitles; material cited from another source is also given as published, with possible errors or misprints indicated in the usual way. In my own text I have used the Canadian/English standard spelling. I have silently exchanged Arabic numerals for Roman ones in chapter and volume citations.

I have used the new *MLA* format throughout, with some variations to ensure consistency; my intent has been to present all necessary information about citations as clearly as possible. Page references have been kept to a minimum and used to indicate chapter or article locations, rather than specific quotations, to keep the text uncluttered; readers should be able to locate all quotations easily from the references given. Page and chapter references to Middleton citations are given for all works without index.

Part One: Monographs

General References

001 Akrigg, G.P.V. Jacobean Pageant or the Court of James I. New York: Atheneum, 1974 (first published by Harvard University Press in 1962). A general historical guide to the period.

002 Archer, William. The Old Drama and the New: an Essay in Re-Valuation. London: William Heinemann, 1923. A typical early twentieth-century look at Middleton's plays. Finds the plays "transcripts of contemporary life," but too depraved for his taste.

003 Ayres, Philip J. Tourneur: The Revenger's Tragedy. London: Edward Arnold, 1977. A student-focussed study of the play; an appendix (pp. 57-62) reviews the authorship question, from the viewpoint that "Middleton is the most likely, indeed the only likely, author of The Revenger's Tragedy."

Reviewed, in NQ 223 (1978): 80, by L.W. Conolly, who commends it as a "short and coherent study."

004 Bakeless, John. The Tragicall History of Christopher Marlowe. Cambridge, Mass.: Harvard University Press, 1942. 2 vols. Mentions Middleton's Black Book in the discussion of the authorship of Tamburlaine and in discussion of Doctor Faustus; notes other echoes of and allusions to Marlowe in A Game at Chess, A Mad World, My Masters and The Family of Love.

005 Barber, C.L. The Idea of Honour in the English Drama 1591-1700. Goteborg: Gothenburg Studies in English 6, 1957. An extensive discussion of various uses of the word "honour" in English drama; discusses eighteen different connotations. Uses most of Middleton's plays as references, but not Women Beware Women.

006 Bentley, G.E. The Jacobean and Caroline Stage. Oxford: Clarendon, 1967 (corrected edition; first published 1956). Vol. 4 of The English Stage. "Thomas Middleton," pp. 855-911. Gives an extensive list of putative canonical plays and poetry; fixes Middleton's dates at 1580-1627. A standard guide; continuation of Chambers--see 023.

007 ----------. *The Profession of Dramatist in Shakespeare's Time 1590-1642*. Princeton: Princeton University Press, 1971. An "explication of the normal working environments circumscribing the activites of those literary artists who were making their living by working for the London theatres." Notes that Middleton was not an "attached" playwright, but worked for several different companies, and was "a talented and successful writer for the theatres"; discusses *A Game at Chess* as part of a chapter on censorship.

> Reviewed in *TLS* 2 Feb. 1973: 126 ("The Professional Ranks"). The reviewer notes that the book "skilfully sifts the evidence to reconstruct the terms under which these playwrights worked," but objects that Shakespeare is not given special treatment.
>
> Also reviewed, in *SQ* 24 (1973): 474-76, by Franklin B. Williams, Jr., who discusses the contents, which he feels must be called "definitive," but notes the lack of secondary references to other modern studies of professional writers of the time and to bibliographical and textual studies.

008 Berger, Thomas L. and William C. Bradford, Jr. *An Index of Characters in the English Printed Drama to the Restoration*. Englewood, Colorado: Microcard Editions Books, 1975. Based on Greg's *Bibliography of Printed Drama to the Restoration* (1939-57)--it therefore includes all of Middleton's plays except *The Witch*. Contains a useful "finding list" of plays that combines the Greg number, the play's title, the author from *Annals* (see Harbage, revised Schoenbaum, 046), Greg's date of publication, *Annals*' date of production, and the *STC* number of the earliest edition. A helpful guide to which characters are in which plays.

009 Bergeron, David M. *English Civil Pageantry 1558-1642*. Columbia, S.C.: University of South Carolina Press, 1971. An historical and descriptive study of civil pageants; contains numerous references to Middleton's pageants, as well as Chapter 7, "Thomas Middleton" (pp. 179-200), which studies all Middleton's mayoral pageants in detail, especially *The Triumphs of Truth* (1613). Emphasises Middleton's use of imagery and his moral theme, the conflict of light and darkness, which was only "fully dramatically realized" in the 1613 pageant. (For an earlier, more general study, see Withington, 128.)

Reviewed, in NQ 218 (1973): 472-3, by G.R. Hibbard, who describes the book's organisation extensively and notes that the information is "invaluable" and that "the specialist will find it indispensable," while finding it rather repetitious, and inaccurate in dealing with cost inflation.

Also reviewed, in SQ 24 (1973): 476, by Marilyn L. Williamson, who praises the "solid scholarship," notes that the book complements, without supplanting, Withington's work (see 128) and observes that the information helps students extend "their sense of the artistic range of important playwrights," including Middleton.

010 Boas, F.S. An Introduction to Stuart Drama. London: Oxford University Press, 1946. A conservative view of Jacobean drama; examines Middleton and Rowley in Chapter 9, "Dramas of Sex Complication," pp. 220-248. Discusses all the major plays; admires A Trick to Catch the Old One and The Changeling, but finds the rest overloaded with sexual obsession.

011 Borden, William R. The English Dramatic Lyric, 1603-42: a Study in Stuart Dramatic Technique. [Hamden, Conn.]: Archon Books, 1969 (reprint; first published 1951 by Yale University Press). A study of the "incidental lyrics" in Tudor and Stuart plays and their various functions and meanings--for example, characterisation, entertainment, etc. Lists Middleton's dramatic lyrics (pp. 188-93), with the first lines of the lyrics and the situation in which each is used. No index.

012 Bradbrook, Muriel C. The Growth and Structure of Elizabethan Comedy. London: Chatto and Windus, 1973 (new edition; first published 1955). Discusses Middleton and his contemporaries, with an emphasis on the Elizabethan audience for which they wrote. Sees Middleton as a keen observer of the contemporary scene, whose moral qualities come from his irony.

013 ----------. The Rise of the Common Player: a Study of Actor and Society in Shakespeare's England. London: Chatto and Windus, 1962. Discusses the role of actor and audience in the development of Elizabethan drama, "one branch of the flourishing tree of sports and pastimes." Considers the stage history of the "common stages" until their replacement by "coterie" companies; includes Middleton as a coterie playwright who "reached new depths of cynicism in depicting the vices of Londoners."

014 ----------. Themes and Conventions of Elizabethan Drama. Cambridge: Cambridge University Press, 1952. Discusses Women Beware Women and The Changeling in Chapter 9, "Thomas Middleton," pp. 213-39. Examines Middleton's use of imagery and theme and concludes that it is less heavy than that of his contemporaries, because he relies as well "upon action and characterisation in a way which no one else did (except Shakespeare)." Notes also that Middleton's language is full of "implication," showing a "pregnant simplicity." (This chapter is reprinted in Elizabethan Drama, pp. 297-319.) Chapter 7, "Cyril Tourneur", contains an analysis of The Revenger's Tragedy which focusses on theme, construction, and language and does not enter the authorship controversy.

014a----------. Themes and Conventions of Elizabethan Tragedy, Second Edition. Cambridge: Cambridge University Press, 1980. The Middleton chapter is pages 206-239, but unchanged. This edition includes a new chapter on performance and an updated (to 1978) bibliography that contains a very slight Middleton listing.

015 Bowers, Fredson Thayer. Elizabethan Revenge Tragedy 1587-1642. Gloucester, Mass.: Peter Smith, 1959 (first published 1940). A "broad view of the background, the origin, and the chronological development of the Tragedy of Revenge." Discusses The Changeling, A Fair Quarrel, and Women Beware Women as Middleton's revenge plays; also discusses The Revenger's Tragedy. Dates Women Beware Women at 1613.

016 Boyer, Clarence Valentine. The Villain as Hero in Elizabethan Tragedy. New York: Russell and Russell, 1964. A study of the "heroic criminals of Elizabethan tragedy"; contains an extensive discussion of The Revenger's Tragedy (Chapter 10, especially pp. 145-151), with no authorship discussion.

017 Briggs, Katharine Mary. Pale Hecate's Team: an Examination of the Beliefs on Witchcraft and Magic among Shakespeare's Contemporaries and His Immediate Successors. New York: Arno Press, 1977 (reprint; first published 1962 by Routledge and Kegan Paul, London). Finds "a sombre power in Middleton's witch passages," but one far from Shakespeare's poetic power. Discusses the Hecate scenes in Macbeth and rejects Middleton as author; discusses Middleton's The Witch, pp. 77-83. (See also Harris, 047.)

018 Brodwin, Leonora Leet. Elizabethan Love Tragedy 1587-1625. New York: New York University Press, 1971. An historical study of love tragedy, dividing it into three categories, "courtly love," "false romantic love," and "worldly love." Discusses extensively in the first category, The Second Maiden's Tragedy (attributed to Chapman by Brodwin--see also her article, 196), in the second, The Changeling, the "final form" of this type, and in the third, Women Beware Women, Middleton's "culminating moment of tragic awareness." Also mentions The Spanish Gipsy as part of the Middleton canon.

Reviewed in "Passions Primmed," in TLS 29 June 1973: 752. The reviewer comments on "the startling naivete of the critic's moralistic judgments."

Also reviewed, in Renaissance Quarterly 26 (1973): 228-31, by Allan Holaday, who feels that "the book's solid virtues overshadow its defiencies," although he disagrees with the interpretation of A Woman Killed With Kindness (Heywood). He commends the emphasis on "the complexity of the love represented" in the plays discussed.

019 Brooke, Nicholas. Horrid Laughter in Jacobean Tragedy. London: Open Books, 1979. A discussion of tragedies that exploit the "relation of tears to laughter." Examines in detail The Changeling and Women Beware Women, as well as The Revenger's Tragedy; observes that Middleton possessed "the subtlest moral intelligence of the Jacobeans" and was "the most controlled artist," who, in Women Beware Women "even more than in The Changeling," demonstrated "the absurdity of worshipping tragedy as a moral force."

020 Camoin, Francois Andre. The Revence [sic] Convention in Tourneur, Webster and Middleton. Salzburg, 1972. Discusses the Jacobean attitude towards revenge; sees Middleton's revenge tragedies as "morally neutral" plays in which the revenger and his victim's damnation or salvation is irrelevant--Middleton's God is "secular," outside man's moral life.

021 Cawley, Robert Ralston. The Voyagers and Elizabethan Drama. Boston: D.C. Heath, 1938 (Monograph Series of the Modern Language Association of America). A study of the impact of the explorers and of travellers' tales on Elizabethan drama; divided into area examined (Egypt, Tartary). Traces references in plays; discusses elements in the majority of Middleton's works.

022 Cazamian, Louis. The Development of English Humour. Durham, N.C.: Duke University Press, 1961. Discusses Middleton in Chapter 13, "Humor in Elizabethan Drama," pp. 337-40. Sees him as "realistic and cynical," with "verve" but little sentimentality or moralizing.

023 Chambers, E.K. The Elizabethan Stage. Oxford: Clarendon, 1951 (corrected edition; first published 1923). (Vol. 3 of The English Stage.) "Thomas Middleton," pp. 437-444. A standard reference work, now somewhat out of date but still very useful as a general reference. Ends with 1613; continuation is in Bentley--see 006.

024 Champion, Larry S. Tragic Patterns in Jacobean and Caroline Drama. Knoxville: University of Tennessee Press, 1977. A study of how dramatic tragedy "reflects the period of political and philosophical transition." Discusses The Revenger's Tragedy (accepts Tourneur as author), Women Beware Women (Middleton's "dispassionate and realistic observation of a viciously corrupt society") and The Changeling, the last two in Chapter 6 (pp. 152-179). Concludes Chapter 6 with the observation that Middleton "has captured amidst his broad scene of societal corruption and tragedy the sheer loneliness and isolation of its victims." (See also his article on Women Beware Women, 211.)

Reviewed, in MLR 76 (1981): 66, by Philip Edwards, who notes that the choice of plays considered is a "familiar selection" that limits the book's argument to familiar territory.

025 Clark, Andrew. Domestic Drama: a Survey of the Origins, Antecedents and Nature of the Domestic Play in England 1500-1640. Salzburg, 1975. 2 vols. A "full-length critical survey" (in part an elaboration and response to Adams's English Domestic or Homiletic Tragedy); includes references to A Yorkshire Tragedy (sometimes--Lake, 147--attributed to Middleton), The Honest Whore (which shows "the vitriolic pen of Dekker's collaborator," probably Middleton; discussed pp. 311-317), A Fair Quarrel (pp. 343-6), and Women Beware Women (pp. 346-55; the final masque "destroys the effect Middleton has already created and does violence to his art"; a "regression to sensational melodrama," it harms his study of a disintegrating marriage).

026 Clarkson, Paul S. and Clyde T. Warren. The Law of Property in Shakespeare and the Elizabethan Drama. Baltimore: Johns Hopkins Press, 1942. A thorough study, by two lawyers, of Elizabethan property law "as illustrated by dramatic passages" from Elizabethan and Jacobean plays; contains many references to Middleton's plays, included in a helpful "index to dramatic citations" (pp. 326-239 for Middleton, one of the longest entries). (See also Johansson, 057.)

027 Colman, E.A.M. The Dramatic Use of Bawdy in Shakespeare. London: Longman, 1974. A consideration of the various meanings of Elizabethan bawdy jokes and puns; while concentrating on Shakespearean usage, the introduction gives a general guide that is helpful when reading Middleton's plays. Phrases are defined and an origin given, and degree of intensity is explained. (For non-Shakespearean bawdy, see Henke, 050.)

028 Cornelia, Maria. The Function of the Masque in Jacobean Tragedy and Tragicomedy. Salzburg, 1978. A discussion of the "dramatic function" of the masque; discusses The Changeling (pp. 120-24), Women Beware Women (pp. 79-82; an "ironic wedding masque") and The Revenger's Tragedy (pp. 82-91; a "danse macabre"). No index is provided. (See also Shaw, 101 and Sutherland, 113.)

029 Curry, John V. Deception in Elizabethan Comedy. Chicago: Loyola University Press, 1955. A detailed study of disguise plots and trickery in comedy; studies types of tricksters and their victims, and the various methods used. A helpful guide to plot intricacies, although the idea remains within the comic framework and no mention is made of the tragic potential in ironic plots. (See also Freeburg, 039.)

030 Doran, Madeleine. Endeavors of Art: a Study of Form in Elizabethan Drama. Madison: University of Wisconsin Press, 1954. Historical criticism, useful in placing Middleton in his period, especially as regards the moral "tags" and open moralizing in the plays; suggests Middleton's morality is a convention, not to be taken very seriously.

031 Downer, Alan S. The British Drama: a Handbook and Brief Chronicle. New York: Appleton-Century-Crofts, 1950. A "guide and companion to those undertaking for the first time a study of the drama." Discusses Middleton's comedy (pp. 142-6) as that of "the generally acknowledged master of Jacobean realistic comedy," and The Changeling as "the greatest tragedy of the period" (discussed pp. 172-4).

032 Eliot, T.S. Elizabethan Dramatists. London: Faber, 1963 (essay written in 1927). Discusses Middleton in "Thomas Middleton," pp. 83-93; sees him as the "great observer" and "great recorder," with his greatest comic character Moll, the Roaring Girl, and his greatest tragedy The Changeling, surpassed by "one Elizabethan alone ... Shakespeare." The Middleton essay appears as well in TLS 30 June 1927: 444-5 (anonymous review article), For Lancelot Andrewes (1928), Elizabethan Essays (1934) and Selected Essays (1932 and 1950). (See also his discussion of the authorship of The Revenger's Tragedy, 260.)

033 Ellis-Fermor, Una. The Jacobean Drama: an Interpretation. London: Methuen, 1965 (fourth edition; revised 1958 and 1961). A comprehensive study; discusses Middleton (in Chapter 7, pp. 128-152) as the "great observer" (quoted from Eliot; see previous item), whose "pitiless abstemiousness" from any pity or sentimentality leads him to belittle human beings. The book discusses The Revenger's Tragedy as part of the Tourneur canon.

034 Empson, William. Some Versions of Pastoral. London: Chatto and Windus, 1935. A survey of some themes in English drama. Discusses the idea of "the changeling", with reference to both The Changeling and Women Beware Women.

035 Everitt, E.B. The Young Shakespeare: Studies in Documentary Evidence. Copenhagen: Rosenkilde & Bagger, 1954. (Anglitica, Vol. 2.) Discusses a theory of Shakespeare as a law clerk; finds evidence for his handwriting in the manuscript of The Second Maiden's Tragedy (Lansdowne 807) and suggests that the manuscript is Shakespeare "chiefly inscribing for Middleton" a collaborative play. (Discussed in her edition of Second Maiden by Anne Lancashire, who finds the theory "implausible" (on p. 72, n. 132).

036 Farley-Hills, David. The Comic in Renaissance Comedy. London: Macmillan, 1981. A critical study of comedies; argues for a "deeply moral Middleton" in "A Satire against Mankind: Middleton's A Mad World, My Masters" (pp. 81-107) and "The Comedy of Good Cheer: Dekker's Shoemaker's Holiday and Collaborations with Middleton" (pp. 108-146). Stresses Middleton's "pessimistic" view of the world and his "Calvinistic" qualities, calls Mad World "the comedy of evil," and credits Middleton with the invention of the shrewd and unsentimental Moll of Roaring Girl; she, like Middleton, has "no illusions about the depravity of the world."

Reviewed, in MP 81 (1984): 415-27, by Standish Henning, who observes, "this book is so filled with errors, unsupported assertions, questionable judgments, and apparent misreadings as to make it unacceptable as trustworthy scholarship or criticism."

Also reviewed, in "Recent Studies in Elizabethan and Jacobean Drama," SEL 22 (1982): 357, by J.L. Styan, who finds the Dekker-Middleton chapter "illuminating" but questions Farley-Hills's analysis of A Mad World, noting that "the author seems to question his own responses about the negative impact of the play."

037 Farnham, William. The Medieval Heritage of Elizabethan Tragedy. Berkeley: University of California Press, 1936. A useful and detailed guide to the background of Elizabethan tragedy; discusses the changing conception of earthly justice and retribution that influenced revenge tragedy and tragedy in general.

038 Ford, Boris, ed. The Age of Shakespeare. Vol. 2 of The New Pelican Guide to English Literature. London: Penguin Books, 1982 (previous edition 1955). Multiple passim references to Middleton; "Middleton's Tragedies," by John H. Jump (pp. 457-70) discusses his tragedies in some depth, commenting that "Middleton's significant, often ironical, juxtaposition of character, speech, and events and his lucid, flexible, highly dramatic but always unobtrusive verse" make his tragedies "among the age's greatest achievements in drama." The article on Tourneur is by L. G. Salingar ("Tourneur and the Tragedy of Revenge", pp. 436-56), and argues that, as far as authorship of The Revenger's Tragedy goes, "with Tourneur, then, rests the benefit of the doubt," largely because changing the attribution to Middleton would "raise problems of artistic continuity" in Middleton's own work.

039 Freeburg, Victor Oscar. Disguise Plots in Elizabethan Drama: a Study in Stage Tradition. New York: Columbia University Press, 1915. A discussion of various disguise plots; mentions Middleton's plays passim, especially Michaelmas Term, A Mad World, My Masters, and The Phoenix. Covers essentially the same ground as Curry (029).

040 Frost, D.L. The School of Shakespeare: the Influence of Shakespeare on English Drama 1600-42. Cambridge: Cambridge University Press, 1968. Discusses Middleton as "Shakespeare's True Heir" (pp. 23-76), arguing that Middleton was a highly imitative playwright, with little personal moral sense, who borrowed some specific elements from Shakespeare (in The Family of Love especially) but was more indebted to Shakespeare for his "revolution in mid career"; argues that Middleton began "suddenly" to interest "himself in the inner workings of the mind" as a result of coming under Shakespeare's influence when he joined the King's Men about 1615. Argues further that in The Changeling, "the influence of Shakespeare reaches its climax and its justification ... for the first and last time Middleton ... achieved a Shakespearean tragedy, a self-consistent and developing study of personal relationships." Discusses the authorship of The Revenger's Tragedy (he finds Middleton's "case" much stronger than Tourneur's "now very shaky" one) and the relationship between the Hecate scenes of Macbeth and The Witch in extensive appendices.

Reviewed in Shakespeare Studies 5 (1969): 325-29 by Charles R. Forker, who notes Frost's "irritatingly categorical chapter titles," discussing the Middleton chapter in detail. Observes that Frost patronises Shakespeare's contemporaries, seeming to feel that "the master" can do no wrong but lesser dramatists no right unless they copy him. Praises the bibliography.

Also reviewed in SQ 20 (1969): 474-75 by Clifford Leech, who also notes Frost's unwillingness to accept that Shakespeare's contemporaries who "strongly responded to him" were "nevertheless men of independent mind who made plays of an individual quality."

041 Gibbons, Brian. Jacobean City Comedy: a Study of Satiric Plays by Jonson, Marston and Middleton. London: Rupert Hart-Davis, 1968. Examines the roots and themes of city comedy; sees it as strongly connected with the rising capitalist class, and divided between "Jacobean" pessimism and "Early Seventeenth Century" optimism. Discusses The Phoenix, A Mad World, My Masters and A Chaste Maid in Cheapside in detail, in Chapter 8, "Middleton and Jonson."

041a----------. Jacobean City Comedy, Second Edition. London and New York: Methuen, 1980. Makes changes to Chapters 1, 4, 5, 6 and 9, to make the book more accessible to non-specialists; no special changes to the chapter on Middleton, now pages 121-138.

042 Greg, W.W. English Literary Autographs 1550-1650. Oxford: Oxford University Press, 1932 (reprinted by Kraus Reprint [Liechtenstein], 1968). Gives a biography of Middleton and some facsimiles of his autograph on page 94 and accompanying plate.

043 Gurr, Andrew. The Shakespearean Stage 1574-1642. Cambridge: Cambridge University Press, 1970. A useful, detailed and illustrated guide to the companies, players, theatres and theatrical conventions and techniques of the Elizabethan and Jacobean stage.

> Reviewed, in NQ 218 (1973): 148, by Philip Edwards, who finds it "full, lively, up-to-date and well-rounded," with a few "moments of irritation" but, "all told," a "helpful and informative book."

044 Hallett, Charles A. and Elaine S. The Revenger's Madness: A Study of Revenge Tragedy Motifs. Lincoln: University of Nebraska Press, 1980. Discusses various revenge themes and motifs; emphasises the cynics in Middleton's plays (see his monograph on Middleton's Cynics, 143) and argues that, in Women Beware Women and The Changeling, Middleton borrows the motifs but not the themes of the revenge play. Discusses The Revenger's Tragedy extensively; argues against Middleton's authorship and calls the "anonymous" author "Tourneur" for convenience, but observes that "in a characteristically Middletonian fashion, Vindice is moved to overreach himself."

> Reviewed, in "Recent Studies in Elizabethan and Jacobean Drama," SEL 22 (1982): 356, by J.L. Styan, who finds it "altogether an interesting treatment of a key genre."

045 Harbage, Alfred. Shakespeare and the Rival Traditions. New York: Macmillan, 1952. An important work on the dual theatre, public and private, of the Jacobean period, with useful information on the coterie theatre in which much of Middleton's drama was performed. Now considered somewhat overstated, but still a useful and important source.

046 ----------, ed.; revised by Samuel Schoenbaum. Annals of English Drama 975-1700. London: Methuen, 1964. With Supplements, ed. S. Schoenbaum. Evanston, Illinois: Department of English, Northwestern University, 1966 and 1970. A comprehensive guide to the stage history of each play of the period covered. A useful guide to play dating, although somewhat controversial in parts. The Supplements make some changes in the dating of Middleton's plays, particularly No Wit No Help Like a Woman's and A Chaste Maid in Cheapside.

047 Harris, Anthony. Night's Black Agents: Witchcraft and Magic in Seventeenth-Century English Drama. Manchester: Manchester University Press, 1980. An extensive and detailed discussion of witch plays; includes an analysis of The Witch ("The Tune of Damnation: Squalid Grandeur in The Witch"; pp. 78-89) that discusses as well the relationship among the Macbeth Hecate scenes, The Witch, and Jonson's Masque of Queenes. (See also Briggs, 017.)

048 Harrison, G.B. A Jacobean Journal, being a record of those things most talked of during the years 1603-1604. London: Routledge, 1946. An entertaining guide to events in London, many of which found their way into Middleton's plays. Includes a mention of the "Triumphal Progress [of James and court] through London," where, at the sixth gate, they met a pageant "written by Thomas Middleton" (15 March 1603/4).

049 Heilman, Robert Bechtold. Tragedy and Melodrama: Versions of Experience. Seattle and London: University of Washington Press, 1968. An "essay" on generic form; discusses The Changeling and The Revenger's Tragedy (as an example of Tourneur's method with melodrama). Argues that Beatrice "takes not only the unusual step from victimizer to victim, but the rare step up from the victim of disaster to the tragic heroine"; notes that Revenger's Tragedy is "a turbulent confluence of different generic tendencies."

050 Henke, James T. Renaissance Dramatic Bawdy (Exclusive of Shakespeare): an Annotated Glossary and Critical Essays. Salzburg, 1974. 2 vols. Volume 2 is the glossary; volume 1 includes an essay on "Bawdy and Comic Satire in Middleton's A Trick to Catch the Old One," pp. 57-79. Argues that Middleton uses "ironic bawdy" to "tighten dramatic structure ... to reveal the inherent stupidity or intelligence of his characters, and finally to render moral judgment." (For more bawdy, see Colman, 027.)

051 Herrick, Marvin T. Tragicomedy: its Origin and Development in Italy, France, and England. Urbana: University of Illinois Press, 1955 (Illinois Studies in Language and Literature, Vol. 39). Discusses the development of "tragedy with a happy ending"; finds Middleton a playwright of "startling contrasts" in tragedy and comedy. Gives a full discussion of Hengist, King of Kent, The Phoenix, A Fair Quarrel, and The Witch.

052 Hibbard, G.R., ed. The Elizabethan Theatre VI: Papers given at the Sixth International Conference on Elizabethan Theatre held at the University of Waterloo, Ontario, in July 1975. Toronto: Macmillan (Canada), 1975. Includes two articles on The Revenger's Tragedy, "On Marston, The Malcontent, and The Revenger's Tragedy," by R.A. Foakes (pp. 59-75), and "The Revenger's Tragedy Revived," by Stanley Wells (pp. 88-133; reviews of productions, chiefly by the Royal Shakespeare Company in 1966-69). For Hibbard's article in this collection, see 303.

053 Hoy, Cyrus. The Hyacinth Room: an Investigation into the Nature of Comedy, Tragedy, and Tragicomedy. New York: Knopf, 1964. A generic study; Middleton is discussed in Chapter 7, "Reason Overthrown," with other Jacobean dramatists. Notes the lack of an ideal in Jacobean drama; observes that in The Changeling, "tragedy, folly and vice imply each other" (p. 273). Discusses as well Women Beware Women, A Chaste Maid in Cheapside, and The Revenger's Tragedy.

054 Jacobson, Daniel Jonathan. The Language of The Revenger's Tragedy. Salzburg, 1974. Summarises the authorship debate; decides to treat the play as anonymous. Studies the language of the play--irony, wordplay, imagery, figurative language--extensively, with a line index.

055 Jewkes, Wilfred T. Act Division in Elizabethan and Jacobean Plays 1583-1616. Hartford, Conn.: Shoe String Press, 1958. An extensive study of "the varied practice of act division." Gives a general discussion and detailed textual studies of specific plays, including most of Middleton's plays that are dated before 1616.

056 Jochum, Klaus Peter. Discrepant Awareness: Studies in English Renaissance Drama. Frankfurt: Peter Lang, 1979. A discussion of the difference between audience and character awareness in drama; notes the surprises for the audience in The Changeling (pp. 248-51) and the different and changing layers of awareness for both audience and characters (and incidentally argues against Middleton's authorship of The Revenger's Tragedy).

057 Johansson, Bertil. Law and Lawyers in Elizabethan England as Evidenced in the Plays of Ben Jonson and Thomas Middleton. Stockholm: Almqvist & Wiksell, 1967. An outline of the court system and practices, with quotes from contemporary literature, as well as a discussion of the attitude towards justice and injustice in Jonson's and Middleton's plays--officers are satirised and lawyers criticised. (See also Clarkson and Warren, 026.)

058 ----------. Religion and Superstition in the Plays of Ben Jonson and Thomas Middleton. Uppsala, 1950. Discusses the uses of religious and superstitious themes in Jonson's and Middleton's plays: Roman Catholicism, Anglicanism, and Protestantism; and magic, astrology, alchemy and witchcraft. A comprehensive study, but no special conclusions.

059 Kernan, Alvin. The Cankered Muse: Satire of the English Renaissance. New Haven: Yale University Press, 1959. A generic study of satire focussed on Elizabethan satire; offers some discussion of Micro-Cynicon and The Black Book, noting that both consider the "satyr's moral hypocrisy." Mentions The Phoenix and Your Five Gallants as plays with characters who are "at least partially satirists"; Middleton is described as one of the "theatrical entrepreneurs ... who were willing to capitalize on any theatrical convention without concern for its possible serious implications." Discusses The Revenger's Tragedy at length (this part of the book is reprinted as "Tragical Satire and The Revenger's Tragedy" in Shakespeare's Contemporaries, pp. 317-327).

060 Kirsch, Arthur C. Jacobean Dramatic Perspectives. Charlottesville: University Press of Virginia, 1972. Discusses various Jacobean themes; finds much moral content in Middleton's plays (pp. 75-96), and sees considerable influence from the medival morality play in his work overall.

061 Klein, David. The Elizabethan Dramatists as Critics. New York: Philosophical Library, 1963. A survey of what Elizabethan playwrights said about plays and players; includes several references to Middleton.

062 Knights, L.C. Drama and Society in the Age of Jonson. London: Chatto and Windus, 1937. A standard resource on the social patterns of the Jacobean period as they affected the drama; analyses Middleton, whom he sees as a "transitional" writer, neither aristocratic nor citizen and therefore quite representative of his changing society, in "Middleton and the New Social Classes," pp. 256-69.

063 Knoll, Robert E. Ben Jonson's Plays: An Introduction. Lincoln: University of Nebraska Press, 1964. A discussion of Jonson that compares his works to those of his contemporaries. Middleton's A Trick to Catch the Old One is compared to The Silent Woman, both being variants of the Prodigal Son play (pp. 115-17); "Middleton has united theme and action better even than Jonson" but Jonson's moral position is "lucid," whereas Middleton's is "confused and dark."

064 Kolin, Philip C. The Elizabethan Stage Doctor as a Dramatic Convention. Salzburg, 1975. A study of the stage doctor "as part of a dramatic pattern." Looks specifically at Middleton's A Fair Quarrel (with Rowley), I Honest Whore (with Dekker), and The Changeling (with Rowley); notes that in The Changeling Beatrice's "perverse use of medicine" is contrasted with the literal physician (Alibius) who is "useless or corrupt" and with Isabella, the "one good doctor figure." Concludes that the doctor was a common figure, variously used with numerous functions, an "evolving convention" and "one of the most significant character conventions of the age."

065 Krook, Dorothea. Elements of Tragedy. New Haven and London: Yale University Press, 1969. An inquiry into the "universal principles or elements" of tragedy; finds four main elements in tragedy; examines Women Beware Women (pp. 146-83) and finds the play tragic, of the "low mimetic" type, dealing with bourgeois characters and settings; argues that the play is a study of the "moral degeneration" of characters (Bianca and Leantio) who are initally innocent and who truly suffer. Praises Middleton's use of "forgetfulness" as the fatal weakness of these characters--it is "the most neutral, nonmoral, nonemotional, noncommittal word that the genius of man could have hit upon to express a profound tragic vision."

Reviewed, in ELN 8 (1971): 306-7, by Clifford Leech, who finds the book the work of "a superior and informed mind working on a major problem." He has some arguments with her view of "catharsis" and her "arbitrary" choice of which plays are tragedies.

066 Lancashire, Anne, ed. Editing Renaissance Dramatic Texts, English, Italian, and Spanish: papers given at the eleventh annual Conference on Editorial Problems, University of Toronto, 31 October to 1 November 1975. New York and London: Garland Publishing, 1976. A collection of articles discussing the difficulties of editing Renaissance texts; some discussion of Middleton texts, including the Game at Chess and Witch manuscripts.

067 Lascelles, Mary. Shakespeare's Measure for Measure. London: The Athlone Press of the University of London, 1953. A discussion of Measure for Measure that includes a running comparison with Middleton's The Phoenix, a "significant analogy." Observes that Phoenix is a "mediocre play ... [that] may serve to measure what can, and what cannot, be done without the Shakespearian magic."

068 ----------. Pre-Restoration Stage Studies. Cambridge, Mass.: Harvard University Press, 1927. A study of stages and staging; discusses The World Tost at Tennis (pp. 334-39).

069 Leggatt, Alexander. Citizen Comedy in the Age of Shakespeare. Toronto: University of Toronto Press, 1973. A comprehensive guide to Jacobean city comedy, studying its history, patterns, values, characters, plots and themes. Discusses specifically A Trick to Catch the Old One, A Mad World, My Masters, The Family of Love, The Roaring Girl, Michaelmas Term, and A Chaste Maid in Cheapside; finds Middleton "one of the masters of intrigue comedy" and citizen comedy itself, drama of social morality that moves between "the assertion of morality and the subversion of morality."

> Reviewed, in JEGP 74 (1975): 115-17, by Jean-Pierre Maquerlot, who argues with Leggatt's "overstress[ing]" of the amorality of the "coterie dramatists," including Middleton, but overall finds the work one of "sound scholarship, a fine sense of nuance, and pleasant humor."

070 Levin, Richard. The Multiple Plot in English Renaissance Drama. Chicago: University of Chicago Press, 1971. The book-length compilation, with additions and emendations, of a number of articles that appeared during the sixties (these are listed and annotated in the Articles section, Part Two, 377 to 393). A very clear and useful guide, with the plots categorised and detailed, that discusses most of Middleton's plays.

Reviewed, in SCN 31 (1973): 88-89, by Judd Arnold, who praises Levin's research and coverage and finds the book overall, while marred by some "cumbersome" parts, "an impressive and useful labor."

Also reviewed, in RenD (n.s.) 5 (1972): 237-43, by Alan C. Dessen, who outlines the book, finds Chapter 4 "provocative," laments Levin's "failure to use the visual/theatrical effects built into" a Jacobean play, and suggests further extensions of the study, involving multiple action, rather than merely plot.

Also reviewed, in MLQ 34 (1973): 100-2, by Clifford Leech, who finds it "a most thorough book," argues some points of interpretation of individual plays, but observes overall that the book "should be read by all interested in English Renaissance dramaturgy."

Also reviewed, in Renaissance Quarterly 26 (1973): 224-28, by Samuel Schoenbaum, who gives a detailed discussion of the book, takes exception to some stylistic details, and concludes that it is a "deeply meditated work of criticism and well worth the effort required to digest it."

Also reviewed, in Shakespeare Jahrbuch (Weimar) 109 (1973): 215-217 [in German], by Georg Seehase.

071 Lynch, Kathleen M. The Social Mode of Restoration Comedy. New York: Octagon Books, 1965 (first published by Macmillan in 1926). Discusses the social aspects of Seventeenth-Century comedy; mentions Middleton as "the greatest realist in Elizabethan drama" and emphasises the social conflict in his plays, especially Michaelmas Term, A Trick to Catch the Old One and A Chaste Maid in Cheapside.

Reviewed in TLS 24 Feb. 1927: 122 ("The Growth of Restoration Comedy"). The reviewer praises the book for having "helped to the understanding of what Restoration comedy can tell about life."

072 Manifold, J.S. The Music in English Drama: from Shakespeare to Purcell. London: Rockcliff, 1956. Discusses "the musical resources and the theatrical conventions" of the period; notes the various conventions Middleton used, including processions in Women Beware Women and funerals in A Chaste Maid in Cheapside and The Old Law.

073 Maxwell, Baldwin. Studies in the Shakespeare Apocrypha. New York: Columbia University King's Crown Press, 1956. Includes studies of The Puritan (pp. 109-37) and A Yorkshire Tragedy (pp. 138-196), including plot summary, dating, analysis of contemporary references and borrowings, and discussion of authorship for both. Argues that Middleton's "must ... be regarded as the principal claim" for Puritan; mentions Oliphant's suggestion of Middleton for Yorkshire Tragedy (see 080).

074 Mehl, Dieter. The Elizabethan Dumb Show: the History of a Dramatic Convention. London: Methuen, 1965. A useful guide to the dumb shows in Elizabethan plays, emphasising their pageant and masque origins. Discusses the dumb shows and masques in Your Five Gallants, A Chaste Maid in Cheapside, Women Beware Women and The Changeling.

075 Morsberger, Robert E. Swordplay and the Elizabethan and Jacobean Stage. Salzburg, 1974. Discusses stage conventions, including how to stage sword fights. Mentions The Fair Quarrel [sic] (pp. 49-51) and "the honour of the duel code."

076 Mullany, Peter F. Religion and the Artifice of Jacobean and Caroline Drama. Salzburg, 1977. Examines the "dramatic use of ... religious materials"; sees the religious elements in the plays as providing an additional emotional thrill and a "romantic escape" (following Ellis-Fermor). Gives an extensive discussion of More Dissemblers Besides Women.

077 Murray, Peter B. A Study of Cyril Tourneur. Philadelphia: University of Pennsylvania Press, 1964. Although primarily a study of Tourneur, the chapter specifically on The Revenger's Tragedy, "The Anonymous Revenger's Tragedy" (pp. 144-257), considers the various alternatives for its authorship and, while leaning strongly towards Middleton, leaves the question open, while giving a reasonable and detailed examination of the play itself.

Reviewed by G.R. Proudfoot in NQ 212 (1967): 233-37. He notes Murray's "indecisiveness" over The Revenger's Tragedy authorship, points out some weaknesses in Murray's arguments for Middleton's authorship, and recommends Murray's final verdict of "not proven" for either Tourneur or Middleton.

078 Neale, J.E. Queen Elizabeth I. Penguin Books, 1934. Still a standard popular biography; as background material, a useful, accessible work.

079 Nicoll, Allardyce. British Drama, sixth edition, revised by J.C. Trewin. London: Harrap, 1978 (first published 1925; fifth edition revised 1962). A survey of British drama; discusses Middleton's comedies (pp. 77-8), which show "a darker side of existence," and his tragedies (pp. 90-91), the vigour of which is "vitiated by the combination of the main plot with another plot wholly inappropriate" (The Changeling), and "by a plethora of romantic intrigue" (Women Beware Women). Argues overall that Middleton's "unrelieved blackness ... can pall."

080 Oliphant, E.H.C. The Plays of Beaumont and Fletcher: an Attempt to Determine Their Respective Shares and the Shares of Others. New York: Phaeton, 1970 (reprint; first published 1927). Discusses, among others, Middleton and his contribution to various Beaumont-Fletcher plays, including The Nice Valor, Wit at Several Weapons, and The Widow, all of which he attributes to Middleton, and suggests that A Yorkshire Tragedy, The Revenger's Tragedy, and The Second Maiden's Tragedy could all be Middleton's.

081 Oras, Ants. Pause Patterns in Elizabethan and Jacobean Drama: an Experiment in Prosody. Gainesville: University of Florida Press, 1960 (University of Florida Monographs/Humanities/No. 3). An examination of a specific aspect of Renaissance verse, "the phenomenon of pauses." A statistical analysis, illustrated by graphs, that is often cited in the controversy over the authorship of The Revenger's Tragedy, because it finds that Revenger's and Atheist's Tragedy "seem to have nothing in common" in this area.

082 Ornstein, Robert. The Moral Vision of Jacobean Tragedy. Madison: University of Wisconsin Press, 1960. Discusses dramatists "caught between old and new ways of determining the realities upon which moral values rest"; considers Middleton (pp. 170-99) "ironically detached" and the possessor of "total indifference to the ideal in human nature," a writer who astringently dissects illusions and shams.

083 Parrott, Thomas Marc and Robert Hamilton Ball. A Short View of Elizabethan Drama. New York: Scribner, 1943. An overview of Middleton in his period; a reasonably standard work. Discusses Middleton in "Later Comedy, Satiric and Realistic," pp. 152-81; finds him a "dispassionate observer of things as they are," cynical about sexual matters.

084 Partridge, A.C. Orthography in Shakespearean and Elizabethan Drama: a Study of Colloquial Contractions, Elision, Prosody and Punctuation. London: Edward Arnold, 1964. A definition and study of orthography; contains, in Appendix V, an essay on "The Orthographical Characteristics of Ralph Crane," the scribe for extant manuscripts of The Witch and A Game at Chess (pp. 172-74).

085 Peery, William. The Plays of Nathan Field. Austin: University of Texas Press, 1950. While a study of a contemporary of Middleton, the introduction includes much comment on Middleton himself, emphasising his "realism," and his goal of "amusement," rather than moral improvement. It is interesting to note how far afield the "traditional" view of Middleton had travelled, even as the Middleton critics themselves were changing their minds.

086 Pendry, E.D. Elizabethan Prisons and Prison Scenes. Salzburg, 1974. 2 vols. An extensive discussion of prisons, actual and dramatic. Chapters 8 to 10 (vol. 2, pp. 264ff) include studies of several of Middleton's plays.

087 Peter, John. Complaint and Satire in Early English Literature. Oxford: Clarendon, 1956. A study of "the nature and quality of early English Satire," its development, and its effect on the drama; ends with 1611. Discusses Micro-Cynicon (pp. 147-48) and The Changeling; devotes a chapter (Chapter 9) to "Tourneur's Tragedies," including The Revenger's Tragedy, whose ascription to Tourneur he suggests has been "vindicated."

088 Potter, Robert. The English Morality Play: Origins, History and Influence of a Dramatic Tradition. London: Routledge and Kegan Paul, 1975. A comprehensive study of the morality tradition and its influence on Elizabethan drama. Includes discussion of a great many moralities and early Tudor plays, as well as the application of morality themes and characteristics to Shakespeare's and Jonson's work. A very useful background guide to the influence on the morality on Middleton plays, although he is not specifically mentioned.

089 Reed, Robert Rentoul, Jr. The Occult on the Tudor and Stuart Stage. Boston: The Christopher Publishing House, 1965. Contains a study of The Witch (pp. 171-76) and other references to Middleton's plays, including The Changeling. Argues that Witch is "the most informative play of the period" on the types of "contemporary witchcraft," although not a particularly effective play.

090 Rhodes, Neil. Elizabethan Grotesque. London, Boston and Henley: Routledge and Kegan Paul, 1980. A study of "the nature of the grotesque in the new styles of comic prose which developed during the 1590s and ... made a considerable impact upon the drama." Discusses Middleton's Black Book (pp. 57-60) and Father Hubburd's Tale (60-61), as well as looking at his use of the "grotesque theme" of "the conflict between the fat and the lean" in Blurt, Master Constable, The Family of Love, and A Chaste Maid in Cheapside.

Reviewed by J.L. Styan in "Recent Studies in Elizabethan and Jacobean Drama", SEL 22 (1982): 358-9, who calls it "an uncomfortable book" but "a well-researched study in style."

091 Ribner, Irving. The English History Play in the Age of Shakespeare. New York: Barnes and Noble, 1965 (revised edition). A study of the development of the English history play; includes a discussion of Hengist, King of Kent, with the comment that Middleton had "little concern for his subject matter as history and ... little true historical purpose", while the subplot is full of "middle class London flavour," like his city comedies. One of the few considerations of Middleton's only history play (sometimes treated as a tragedy instead).

092 ----------. Jacobean Tragedy: the Quest for Moral Order. London: Methuen, 1962. Discusses Jacobean tragedy as reflecting "the undertainty of an age no longer able to believe in the old ideals" but still maintaining Christian orientation. Considers Middleton in Chapter 6 (pp. 123-52); finds him "fully Christian. ... His moral categories are clear and precise [but] ... his vision is one of hell and damnation." He also finds Middleton realistic in his portrayal of London and of psychology.

093 Ricks, Christopher, ed. English Drama to 1710. London: Sphere Books, 1971. Vol. 3 of The Sphere History of Literature in the English Language. Includes as essay on "Elizabethan and Jacobean Drama" by Brian Morris (pp. 91-94 on Middleton) and "The Tragedies of Webster, Tourneur and Middleton: Symbols, Imagery and Conventions" by Christopher Ricks (pp. 306-349). Morris notes that "Middleton's so-called 'realism' is an elusive quality" and that the playwright shows "distorted lives chronicled unflinchingly." Ricks argues that "linked significances, imagery, themes, symbols, and conventions are all secondary to plot and character" and assesses the plays accordingly, praising Middleton's ability to integrate conventional images and attitudes into the overall "psychological and moral purposes" of his plays, particularly in The Changeling.

094 Ristine, Frank Humphrey. English Tragicomedy: its Origin and History. New York: Russell and Russell, 1963 (first published 1910). Discusses briefly A Fair Quarrel, The Spanish Gipsy, and The Witch as forays into tragicomedy by playwrights of "realistic and domestic drama," in "The Heyday of English Tragicomedy (1610-1642)," especially pp. 124-130.

095 Rossiter, Arthur Percival. English Drama from Early Times to the Elizabethans: its Background, Origins and Developments. London: Hutchinson's University Library, 1950. A survey of English drama, concentrating on the influence of the morality tradition. Concludes that "above all, the characteristic English mode was a mixed one," including elements from varied sources.

096 Saloman, Brownell. Critical Analyses in English Renaissance Drama: a Bibliographic Guide. Bowling Green, Ohio: Bowling Green University Popular Press, 1979. (**Popular School Update and Books in Print)

097 Schelling, Felix E. Elizabethan Playwrights: a Short History of the English Drama from Mediaeval Times to the Closing of the Theaters in 1642. New York: Benjamin Blom, 1965 (first published by Harper in 1925). A survey of Elizabethan drama; discusses the "coarseness and uncleanness" with which Middleton details "the seamy side of London life."

098 ----------. Foreign Influences in Elizabethan Plays. New York and Evanston: Harper and Row, 1969 (first published 1923). A study of foreign settings and their connotations in various plays; discusses the use of Italian and Spanish settings in Middleton's plays, using The Changeling as an example of an Italian setting.

099 Schoenbaum, Samuel. Internal Evidence and Elizabethan Dramatic Authorship: an Essay in Literary History and Method. Evanston: Northwestern University Press, 1966. Discusses the various methods of attribution by internal evidence; a sensible and rather sceptical introduction to the intricacies of such attribution. Includes an evaluation of the evidence for Middleton's authorship of The Revenger's Tragedy; decides to leave it anonymous (a change of mind--see his monograph on Middleton's Tragedies, 152).

Reviewed, in NQ 212 (1967): 238-9, by John J. Jump, who comments that the book "will certainly help to introduce a little order into an area which has not so far been remarkable for it," but objects to Schoenbaum's total denial of the value of intuition to authorship discussions.

100 Scott, Michael. Renaissance Drama and A Modern Audience. London: Macmillan, 1982. A work intended to introduce the reader to "the modernity inherent in seven seminal plays," including The Revenger's Tragedy (pp. 31-46) and The Changeling (pp. 76-88). Argues that De Flores' outsider quality makes him "existential," while Beatrice is a "product of the mercantile society in which she lives"; notes details of modern stage productions and their effects.

101 Shaw, Catherine M. "Some Vanity of Mine Art": the Masque in English Renaissance Drama. Salzburg, 1979. An exhaustive study of Renaissance English masques in drama; discusses a number of Middleton's plays, including Game at Chess (pp. 558-62). No index is provided. (See also Cornelia, 028, and Sutherland, 113.)

> Reviewed, in Cahiers Elisabethains 22 (1982): 132, by Francois Laroque, who finds the book useful, and recommends it as a complement to Cornelia's work (028).

102 Shepherd, Simon. Amazons and Warrior Women: Varieties of Feminism in Stuart-Caroline Drama. Brighton, Sussex: Harvester Press, 1981. A discussion of the "warrior woman," who "fights the men of whom she disapproves," verbally or morally as well as physically. Discusses, among various references to Middleton's sympathy for women, The Family of Love, The Ghost of Lucrece, A Mad World, My Masters, Michaelmas Term, and particularly The Roaring Girl (74-83). (See also his edition of The Family of Love, 605.)

103 Sibley, Gertrude Marian. The Lost Plays and Masques 1500-1642. Ithaca: Cornell University Press, 1933. Descriptions, as full as possible, of lost plays and masques; includes those plays and masques attributed to Middleton as well as a number of plays mentioned in The Mayor of Quinborough (Bullen edition vol. 2, p. 93).

> Mentioned by Clifford Leech, in Renaissance Quarterly 26 (1973), p. 366, as "a most useful reference work for nearly forty years."

104 Smith, Hallett. Elizabethan Poetry: a Study in Convention, Imagery, and Expression. Cambridge, Mass.: Harvard University Press, 1952. A general study of poetry in the Elizabethan period; mentions The Ghost of Lucrece (p. 126) and makes several allusions to Micro-Cynicon, both Middleton's early work.

105 Spencer, Theodore. Death and Elizabethan Tragedy: a Study of Convention and Opinion in the Elizabethan Drama. New York: Pageant Books, 1960. An attempt to "define the attitudes toward death" in the Elizabethan-Jacobean era, and to "show how they affected dramatic poetry"; makes passim references to Middleton throughout.

106 Spens, Janet. Elizabethan Drama. New York: Russell and Russell, 1970 (reprint; first published 1922). Discusses Middleton as one of "The Decadents," pp. 131-141. States that Middleton is chiefly remembered for A Fair Quarrel and The Changeling (pp. 134-37) and that he gives the impression of "the essential fineness of his own standards" even in Changeling and Women Beware Women.

107 Stagg, Louis C. The Figurative Language of Shakespeare's Chief Seventeenth-Century Contemporaries: an Index. New York: Garland, 1982. A collection of the separate indices he has compiled, including one on Heywood and one on Middleton. (Books in Print and Garland catalogue.)

108 Stavig, Mark. John Ford and the Traditional Moral Order. Madison: University of Wisconsin Press, 1968. Examines the plays of Ford and his predecessors, including Middleton. Finds the Jacobean theory of tragedy moral, but notes that theories do not always fit the plays: "the form came first and then the theory." Sees Middleton as a "stoic," advocating endurance and responsibility; concludes that Jacobean theatre did not really represent "a period of moral decadence."

109 Stilling, Roger. Love and Death in Renaissance Tragedy. Baton Rouge: Louisiana State University Press, 1976. A discussion of the "motif" of "the oppostion of love and death" in Elizabethan and Jacobean tragedy; discusses Middleton in Chapter 13, pp. 245-265, and passim. Finds Middleton "antiromantic" on the nature of women and love, and best at "bad, vain, or amoral women" and at the "passionate and moving" analysis of the "plight ... of the male in his necessary and inescapable confrontation with these women." Argues against Middleton's authorship of The Revenger's Tragedy because it lacks "characters of any psychological interest."

110 Stodder, Joseph Henry. Satire in Jacobean Tragedy. Salzburg, 1974. A discussion, using many quotes from other critics, of the "effect of satire on Jacobean tragedy" and their blending in "tragic satire"; considers Middleton in Chapter 4 (pp. 132-42), as well as Tourneur (pp. 103-9; briefly considers the authorship question surrounding The Revenger's Tragedy). Finds Middleton's tragic world one not of "tragic satire" but of serious corruption and hence irony.

111 Stone, Lawrence. The Crisis of the Aristocracy 1558-1641. Oxford: Clarendon, 1965. A standard work on the social climate of the Elizabethan-Jacobean period, especially as it involved the conflict between the "landed gentry" and old aristocracy and the rising urban classes--helpful background to Middleton's city comedies. Available as well in an abridged form that is considerably less detailed. Somewhat controversial, but a very useful source.

112 Stroup, Thomas B. Microcosmos: the Shape of the Elizabethan Play. Lexington: University of Kentucky Press, 1965. A study of the use of "the world as stage"; discusses Middleton's use of pageantry, setting, and social order and notes A Game at Chess's use of "a little world" on stage.

113 Sutherland, Sarah P. Masques in Jacobean Tragedy. New York: AMS Press, 1983. A discussion of the use of masques in plays; deals in detail with Women Beware Women (Chapter 7, pp. 87-100) and The Changeling (Chapter 8, pp. 101-111). Argues that Women contains "six dramatic instances of the wicked being snared in a masque of his or her own hands" and discusses the relationship of the word "changes" in The Changeling to the masque of madmen. (See also Cornelia, 028, and Shaw, 101, for further studies of masques in drama.)

114 Sykes, H. Dugdale. Sidelights on Elizabethan Drama: a Series of Studies Dealing with the Authorship of Sixteenth and Seventeenth Century Plays. London: Cass, 1966 (new imprint; first edition Oxford, 1924). Discusses Anything for a Quiet Life (Middleton and Webster), The Spanish Gipsy, and The Revenger's Tragedy and The Second Maiden's Tragedy in the appendix.

115 Symons, Arthur. Studies in the Elizabethan Drama. New York: Dutton, 1919. Reviews various playwrights; finds Middleton's early comedy "light, rancid" and "irresponsible rather than immoral," and suggests that Rowley's influence gave Middleton a capacity for showing "great passions" --The Changeling is noble, but Women Beware Women isn't.

116 Thomas, Sidney. The Antic Hamlet and Richard III. New York: King's Crown Press, 1943. Notes that The Revenger's Tragedy's Vindice, Hamlet and the Vice in medieval comedy all play the "antic" and the "sardonic masker"; finds Vindice closer to the Vice than Hamlet, because he is "much less profoundly developed."

117 Tillyard, E.M.W. The Elizabethan World Picture. London: Chatto and Windus, 1943. A standard overall guide to the Elizabethan outlook; a basic and accessible source for the beginning student of the period.

118 Tomlinson, T.B. A Study of Elizabethan and Jacobean Tragedy. Cambridge: Cambridge University Press, 1964. Studies A Chaste Maid in Cheapside and Women Beware Women, in Chapter 8, "Naturalistic Comedy and Tragedy," pp. 158-84, and The Changeling, in Chapter 9, "Poetic Naturalism"; defines "naturalism" as domestic comedy or tragedy. Finds Middleton detached, an "amused observ[er]," with a flat tone and a general lack of melodrama and hyperbole.

119 Ure, Peter. Elizabethan and Jacobean Drama: Critical Essays by Peter Ure, ed. J.C. Maxwell. Liverpool: Liverpool University Press, 1974. A series of essays revised following Ure's death in 1969. See 549 for his essay on "The Middleton-Dekker Oxymoron," reprinted in this collection on pp. 187-208; an essay on "Marriage and the Domestic Drama in Heywood and Fletcher," pp. 145-65, includes a study of Women Beware Women as "a new kind of domestic drama" that shows "the slow dissolution of the marriage band incarnate in Leantio and Bianca."

Reviewed by G. Bullough in English Studies 58 (1977): 245-47, who commends the range and quality of essays in the collection.

120 Ward. A.W. and A.R. Waller, eds. *The Cambridge History of English Literature*. Cambridge: Cambridge University Press, 1932. Vol. 6. Chapter 3, "Middleton and Rowley," pp. 58-80, surveys Middleton's life and work (an entry that is now rather out of date) and claims that Middleton's "new capacity" for rendering "loftiness in good and evil," shown in *A Fair Quarrel*'s Ager, is the result of Rowley's influence, exhibited again in *The Changeling*.

121 Watson, Harold Francis. *The Sailor in English Fiction and Drama 1550-1800*. New York: AMS Press, 1966. A study of the presentation of the sailor in fiction and drama; mentions Middleton's use of the characters in Chapter 4, "The Sailor in the Drama 1600-1642," especially pp. 89-96. Discusses *The Family of Love*, *The Black Book*, *The Phoenix*, and *The World Tost at Tennis*.

122 Wedgwood, C.V. *Seventeenth-Century English Literature*. London: Oxford University Press, 1970. Second edition, with an updated bibliography. Discusses Middleton in "The Jacobean Age: Drama" (pp. 26-36); comments that Middleton had "a wonderfully quick eye for women's psychology."

123 Wells, Henry W. *Elizabethan and Jacobean Playwrights*. Port Washington, N.Y.: Kennikat Press, 1964 (revised edition; originally published 1939 and 1940). Discusses "mordant, witty, and disillusioned" Middleton's "cunning sense of actuality," and "racy pictures of London"s social life." *Passim* references throughout the book.

124 Welsford, Enid. *The Court Masque*: a Study in the Relationship between Poetry and the Revels. New York: Russell and Russell, 1962 (reprint; first published 1927 by Cambridge University Press). A study of the "English Court masque of the seventeenth century"; in "Jacobean Masque," pp. 168-216, *The Masque of Heroes* and *The World Tost at Tennis* ("the first masque composed for the theatre") are described and discussed.

125 West, Robert Hunter. *The Invisible World*: a Study of Pneumatology in Elizabethan Drama. New York: Octagon Books, 1969 (reprint; first published 1939). A study of Elizabethan and Jacobean ghosts, and related ideas including witchcraft, seen from a contemporary (sixteenth-century) viewpoint; a long "background" section. Discusses *The Changeling*, in which a "persecuting spirit," or perhaps a "work of conscience," is seen in Alonso's ghost in IV and V (p. 177), and also *The Witch*, in which "the witch scenes are but incidental" (p. 158).

126 Wickham, Glynne. *Early English Stages 1300-1660*. Volume 2, 1576-1660; Part 2, 1597-1660. London: Routledge and Kegan Paul, 1972. An historical survey and study of the playhouses and theatres used in the early seventeenth century, and of the manner in which plays were presented; Middleton is mentioned in passing. (Volume 4 is planned to cover "Plays and Their Makers" from 1576.)

> Volume 2 is reviewed, in *NQ* 218 (1973): 146, by Philip Edwards, who notes Wickham's emphasis on the importance of court performance in the development of the playhouse and playing conventions.

127 Wilson, F.P. *Elizabethan and Jacobean*. Oxford: Clarendon, 1945. Discusses Middleton in the chapter on "Drama" (pp. 84-108); finds him "the writer who next to Shakespeare gets the profoundest effects of tragedy with the utmost plainness of speech." (This chapter is reprinted in *Elizabethan Drama*, pp. 3-21.)

128 Withington, Robert. *English Pageantry*: an Historical Outline. New York: Benjamin Blom 1963 (reprint; first published 1918 by Harvard University Press). 2 vols. A full discussion of pageants in English into the twentieth century. Includes a section on "royal entries" in the seventeenth century and on Lord Mayor's Shows and mentions Middleton's contribution to the Royal Entry of 1604, his Lord Mayor's Shows, and *Civitatis Amor* (1616). (For a fuller discussion of Middleton's pageants, see Bergeron, 009.)

129 Young, Alan R. *The English Prodigal Son Plays*: a Theatrical Fashion of the Sixteenth and Seventeenth Centuries. Salzburg, 1979. A study of various themes and plots in English prodigal son plays; discusses the "inverted tradition" of Middleton's *A Trick to Catch the Old One* and *A Mad World, My Masters* (pp. 270-74). (See also Rowe, 151.)

130 Zocca, Louis R. *Elizabethan Narrative Poetry*. Rutgers, New Jersey: Rutgers University Press, 1950. An analysis of narrative poetry; includes a discussion of Middleton's *The Ghost of Lucrece* in Chapter 5 ("Single Mirrors: Classical and Biblical Material," pp. 47-57). One of the few critical considerations of Middleton's poetry.

Monographs concerned specifically with Middleton

131 Asp, Carolyn. *A Study of Thomas Middleton's Tragicomedies*. Salzburg, 1974. Finds in the tragicomedies a "consistent ethical viewpoint" in the continual emphasis on a "personal integrity" that maintains itself despite a world of deceit; in this way, they differ in moral viewpoint from the comedies and tragedies. Discusses *A Fair Quarrel*, *The Old Law*, and *The Witch*.

132 Baines, Barbara Joan. *The Lust Motif in the Plays of Thomas Middleton*. Salzburg, 1973. Discusses the role of sexual lust and the lust for "cash and property" in Middleton's plays; looks at most of the main plays, including *The Spanish Gipsy*. Finds Middleton "objective," with an attitude towards lust typical of "the conservative Christian tradition." An thorough examination of the subject.

133 Balch, Marston Stevens. *A Mad World, My Masters and Three Farces and a Comedy of the Eighteenth Century*. Salzburg, 1981. A discussion of the adapations of Middleton's play in the eighteenth century. Part of a series of brief monographs on adaptations and borrowings from Middleton in the seventeenth and eighteenth centuries (see following entries).

134 ----------. *Middleton's A Trick to Catch the Old One and Massinger's A New Way to Pay Old Debts (1633)*. Salzburg, 1981. Discusses Massinger's possible borrowings from Middleton's play, including a thorough scene-by-scene comparison and a comparison of phraseology. Argues that Massinger's borrowings produced a "superior play" from the same elements.

135 ----------. *Thomas Middleton's No Wit, No Help Like a Woman's and The Counterfeit Bridegroom (1677) and Further Adaptations*. Salzburg, 1980. Discusses the seventeenth-century adaptations of the play, with a bibliography of the adaptations and the "genealogy" of *No Wit, No Help*.

136 ----------. *Thomas Middleton's A Trick to Catch the Old One, A Mad World, My Masters and Aphra Behn's City Heiress*. Salzburg, 1981. Examines in detail Behn's use of material from Middleton's two plays; includes charts and scene-by-scene analysis. (For more adaptations and borrowings, see Hogg, 306-8.)

137 Barker, Richard Hindry. Thomas Middleton. New York: Columbia University Press, 1958. Written several years before publication (about 1943), this remains one of the few book-length studies of the complete Middleton canon; although it predates much of the biographical research that has illuminated Middleton's early works, it provides a survey of canon and attribution. A useful general study with rather brief discussion of individual plays; finds Middleton showing "dispassionate" and "ironic rather than moralistic" qualities in his earlier plays, but taking "a much more serious view of human frailty" in his later work.

138 Britten, Norman A. Thomas Middleton. New York: Twayne, 1972. A general study, with useful play summaries and bibliography; finds Middleton very "modern" in his psychological realism and "astringent, cool manner." Concludes that Middleton is "a highly moral" writer, with "no illusions about sin and no help for those who embrace it."

139 Cherry, Caroline Lockett. The Most Unvaluedst Purchase: Women in the Plays of Thomas Middleton. Salzburg, 1973. Surveys the sources of Christian attitudes towards women and discusses their reflection in Middleton's plays; argues that Middleton was a "realist," whose works "faithfully reproduce what was said and thought about women, the various occupations and courses of action open to them, and some of the forces governing them."

140 Covatta, Anthony. Thomas Middleton's City Comedies. Lewisburg, Pa.: Bucknell University Press, 1973. A comprehensive study of Middleton's comedies; argues that Middleton "revised his own notions of moral conduct" as time went on, but bases this on a rather tenuous acceptance of the order in which the plays were written. Concludes that the endings of the comedies restore order through the triumph of the "fresh" young, "the precision with which ... fate meets particular vice," and the hope of a "staid but pleasant and peaceable world of simple honesty and virtue" that infuses all characters. A much softer view of Middleton than is generally found.

[The various critical viewpoints have had a field day with this study; a selection of their responses follows.]

Reviewed in Renaissance Quarterly 28 (1975): 422-43 by Alan C. Dessen, who comments that "the author's analyses of individual plays are often illuminating, but, in my opinion, he does not do justice to Middleton's finest comedy, A Chaste Maid" and does not really establish his case for a "genial" Middleton.

Also reviewed in RES 28 (1977): 93-95 by Roma Gill, who finds the book "confused."

Also reviewed in JEGP 74 (1975): 113-15 by Jean-Pierre Maquerlot, who argues that "the whole analysis substantiates the final conclusion"; although the study is "not without flaw"--it is inaccurate in the presentation of other critics' viewpoints--on the whole the book is "worth [the reader's] while."

Also reviewed in Shakespeare Quarterly 26 (1975): 313-14 by Gail Kern Paster, who finds the book "a sharp disappointment" and concludes that Middleton's comedies "deserve more ambitious and original treatment."

Also reviewed in PQ 54 (1975): 541-43 by Robert L. Root, Jr., who calls the book a "cautious, carefully constructed study," an "asset to Middleton criticism."

Also reviewed in SCN 32 (1974): 76-77 by Stephen Wigler, who finds the book "unstimulating" and unclear, without any insights that differentiate Middleton's comedies from any other comedy.

141 Farr, Dorothy M. _Thomas Middleton and the Drama of Realism_: a Study of Some Representative Plays. Edinburgh: Oliver and Boyd, 1973. Discusses especially _The Widow_, _A Chaste Maid in Cheapside_, _A Fair Quarrel_, _The Changeling_ and _Women Beware Women_; sees a development in Middleton's moral attitude, which depends largely on _The Changeling_ predating _Women Beware Women_. Finds that "with Middleton, evil is never overcome by good"; his plays show instead the "ironic comedy inherent in human existence" and present an "unfinished achievement" because of his concession to mode in _Women Beware Women_'s final violence.

> Reviewed by S. Gorley Putt, in _TLS_ 2 Aug. 1974: 833-4 ("The Tormented World of Middleton"). See 485.

> Also reviewed by Stephen Wigler in _SCN_ 33 (1975): 63-4, who finds that Farr gives a sensible and useful overview, especially of _A Fair Quarrel_, but misses Middleton's use of the grotesque to "make us recognize in ourselves what we ordinarily suppress" (see his articles, 558-61, for further details on his view of Middleton's "grotesque").

142 Friedenreich, Kenneth, ed. "_Accompaninge the players_": Essays Celebrating Thomas Middleton, 1580-1980. New York: AMS Press, 1983 (AMS Studies in the Renaissance 8). An assortment of essays, on almost every facet of Middleton's art from textual detail to psychology and philosophy, to celebrate the four hundredth anniversary of his birth. (See separate entry for each essay: Bergeron, Brittin, Friedenreich, Gill, Knight, Lancashire, McCanles, Messina, Morrison, Muir, Richman, Shand, Wigler.)

> Reviewed, in "Recent Studies in Elizabethan and Jacobean Drama", _SEL_ 24 (1984): 403-5, by Richard P. Wheeler, who praises the collection's "engaging variety of critical voices, styles, and claims." A full review, with discussion of most of the articles.

143 Hallett, Charles A. Middleton's Cynics: a Study of Middleton's Insight into the Moral Psychology of the Mediocre Mind. Salzburg, 1975. A book-length compilation of his articles on Middleton's plays (see 293-96), with added consideration of the tragicomedies (or "serious plays") and additional comedies and tragedies; discusses Middleton's "telling psychological portrait" of the mediocre cynic. Concludes that Middleton failed as a playwright, although he succeeded as a psychologist, because he continued to write conventional plays and unfortunately "discovered that [mediocre men] was his theme only after writing about them for many years ... ;[then] he demonstrated such a thorough grasp of their psychological make-up that he was able to predict the spiritual collapse of western society."

> Reviewed by Richard Levin in MLR 73 (1978): 396-98; he observes that "the poor comedies must undergo a strange transformation ... they must lose their comicality ... [and] their artistic value as well," as they become like the progress reports of a "graduate student who is taking over twenty years to complete his dissertation."

144 Heinemann, Margot. Puritanism and Theatre: Thomas Middleton and Opposition Drama under the Early Stuarts. Cambridge: Cambridge University Press, 1980. A "look at Thomas Middleton's work in relation to the society and social movements of his time"; also considers Middleton's patrons and the canon of his plays. Includes the discussion of Puritan "opposition" influences and A Game at Chess contained in her article, 300.

> Reviewed, in MLR 79 (1984): 146-47, by Ann Jennalie Cook, who praises the political analysis and the perspective on Middleton's politics and on the Puritans and argues that the book's weakness is the two final chapters, which are not integrated into the work as a whole and show some inaccuracy about Jacobean play presentation.

145 Holmes, David M. The Art of Thomas Middleton: a Critical Study. Oxford: Clarendon, 1970. A thorough study of the Middleton canon; concludes that "Middleton's artistic point of view was conditioned by his humanity and tempered by experience, but it remained fundamentally critical and didactic." Discusses in detail the plays' themes and considers as well the early prose and poetry; accepts Blurt, Master-Constable as Middleton's because of the way it fits into the thematic patterns Holmes finds (see also his article on Blurt, 318).

Reviewed in "Moralising Away the Art of Middleton," in TLS 26 March 1971: 436; the reviewer notes that the chapter on Blurt, Master Constable is "interesting," as Holmes is "the first to explore [the play] seriously," but argues that overall Holmes's "distortion" and narrow focus reduces the plays' dramatic qualities.

Also reviewed, in ELN 10 (1972): 128-29, by Mark Eccles, who finds the book "a naive effort to explain a sophisticated dramatist," written by a "moralizing critic."

Also reviewed, in Shakespeare Studies 9 (1976): 330-34, by Joel H. Kaplan, who finds Holmes's approach limited, as it allows no consideration of Middleton's time, his contemporaries, the conventions of the stage, etc. Finds that Holmes's dependence on Middleton's poetry as his "credo" causes his play analyses to be full of "oversolemnity"; concludes that the book misses the "complexity and richness" of Middleton's work, partly because it omits the pageants.

Also reviewed, in YES 3 (1973): 284-86, by R.B. Parker, who has "serious reservations" about Holmes's approach, its "reductiveness" and "distortion," and finds the book overall "the exegesis of a comic genius by a critic who apparently does not use his sense of humour."

Also reviewed, in Criticism 13 (1972): 90-93, by Leonard Tennenhouse, who finds the book "quite a useful study of Middleton's growth as a dramatist but a somewhat less satisfactory account of Middleton's moral stance," as it fails to emphasise his irony sufficiently.

146 Jackson, MacD[onald], P. Studies in Attribution: Middleton and Shakespeare. Salzburg, 1979. A textual study in attribution, using similar methods to Lake's better known study (following item), and reaching (independently) similar conclusions. Adds The Puritan, The Revenger's Tragedy, Wit at Several Weapons (with Rowley), The Nice Valour (possibly with Fletcher) and The Second Maiden's Tragedy, and subtracts Blurt, Master Constable, The Spanish Gipsy and The Family of Love, as well as suggesting strong evidence for the inclusion of Timon of Athens I.ii and III and A Yorkshire Tragedy. Argues strongly in favour of Middleton's authorship of Revenger's Tragedy; objects that "suspension of judgement on the authorship question ... almost always has the practical result of leaving the play with Tourneur" despite the considerable body of evidence for Middleton's authorship. (His recent edition of the play attributes it to Middleton; see 619.)

147 Lake, David J. The Canon of Thomas Middleton's Plays: Internal Evidence for the Major Problems of Authorship. Cambridge: Cambridge University Press, 1975. A very detailed study of internal evidence, this work raises as many questions as it answers; while not the final word on Middleton authorship problems, it does provide some interesting suggestions and evidence. Enlarges the canon considerably (among others, The Revenger's Tragedy, The Second Maiden's Tragedy, The Yorkshire Tragedy, A Nice Valour, Anything for a Quiet Life, and Wit at Several Weapons are included, the last four as collaborations; Blurt, Master Constable and The Spanish Gipsy are definitely excluded--attributed to Dekker and Dekker with Ford respectively. (See Jackson, previous entry, for parallel arguments.)

Reviewed in MLR 72 (1977): 895-97 by R.A. Foakes, who finds that Lake's "total confidence is in fact one of the disturbing features of the book," inviting as it does a "categorical response" and thus limiting the effectiveness of his research. Argues that Lake neglects "authorial variants" in his study of manuscripts as guides to Middleton's characteristic contractions.

Also reviewed, in JEGP 75 (1976): 414-17, by MacD[onald] P. Jackson, who notes that Lake's conclusions "agree closely with" Jackson's own study. He surveys Lake's research and findings, praises his "sophistication in textual matters" and notes a few omissions. Emphasises Lake's inclusion in the Middleton canon of Revenger's Tragedy and scenes from Timon of Athens.

148 McElroy, John F. *Parody and Burlesque in the Tragicomedies of Thomas Middleton*. Salzburg, 1972. A detailed study of Middleton's tragicomedies that sees these plays as parodies, in which "the comic material serves not to enhance by contrast the romantic ideals ... but sardonically to render judgment on them," of Fletcherian tragicomedy. Argues that all of Middleton's plays, except for some of the satiric comedies, may be seen as parodies, of romantic tragedy, of history plays, of romantic comedy (*Blurt*), and of city comedy (*Chaste Maid*).

149 Mulryne, J.R. *Thomas Middleton*. Harlow, Essex: Longman, 1979. A discussion of Middleton's life and work, including detailed play analyses, with a select annotated bibliography.

150 Nauer, Bruno. *Thomas Middleton: A Study of the Narrative Structures*. Zurich: Juris, 1977. A study of the plot structures in Middleton's plays; argues that the emphasis on ironic juxtaposition points to Middleton's central theme of "human corruption and blindness"; concludes that Middleton's "values and convictions, stated and mirrored in the dramatic structures ... are traditionally Christian, with a certain Calvinist tendency."

151 Rowe, George E., Jr. *Thomas Middleton and the New Comedy Tradition*. Lincoln: University of Nebraska Press, 1979. A development of his articles (498 and 499); discusses Middleton's "revision" of the New Comedy traditions of Latin drama and his undermining of these traditions in order to criticise the assumptions behind them--argues that for Middleton no harmony or reconciliation is possible. (See also Young, 129, for more discussion of the comedy tradition used by Middleton.)

152 Schoenbaum, Samuel. *Middleton's Tragedies*: a Critical Study. New York: Columbia University Press, 1955. A study of the themes of Middleton's tragedies; includes *Hengist, King of Kent* and, after some discussion, *The Revenger's Tragedy* and *The Second Maiden's Tragedy* among them. Finds in the tragedies a parallel to the themes of the comedies; they exhibit Middleton's "characteristic preoccupation with sexual transgression and its essentially ironic consequences." Sees blindness towards sin and moral order as Middleton's main theme, one that is developed through irony in all of his plays. (See also his general study, *Internal Evidence*, 099, and his many articles on specific plays and aspects of plays, 507 to 515.)

Reviewed, in *JEGP* 55 (1956): 316-18, by Mark Eccles, who agrees with Schoenbaum's inclusion of *Revenger's* and *Second Maiden's Tragedy*, and reviews the authorship controversy. He observes that Schoenbaum "overpraises" *Hengist, King of Kent* and regrets that "the least satisfying part of the book is the chapter on Middleton's greatest tragedies."

153 Stagg, Louis C. *An Index to the Figurative Language of Thomas Middleton's Tragedies*. 1970 (**Popular School) See his work on all of Shakespeare's "Chief Seventeenth-Century Contemporaries," 107.

154 Wiggin, Pauline G. *An Inquiry into the Authorship of The Middleton-Rowley Plays*. Boston: Ginn, 1897. A discussion of the collaboration between Middleton and Rowley in *A Fair Quarrel*, *The World Tost at Tennis* (masque), *The Changeling* and *The Spanish Gipsy*. Concludes that Rowley was responsible for the "humane" and "romantic" qualities of these plays, the "respect for human nature, especially for women," and ascribes scenes accordingly.

Part Two: Articles

155 Adams, Henry Hitch. "Cyril Tourneur on Revenge." JEGP 48 (1949): 72-87. Discusses the case for Tourneur's authorship of The Revenger's Tragedy; finds that it and The Atheist's Tragedy together present "a single mind's ordered view of the universe": Revenger's explains "the entire idea of revenge," with nine different revenge motives in the play, and introduces the "man who suffers his wrongs in patience" and is avenged by heaven; Atheist's develops this characterisation through a whole play.

156 Aggeler, Geoffrey. "Irony and Honour in Jacobean Tragedy." Humanities Association Bulletin 18.2 (1967): 8-19. Discusses the "extraordinary popular interest in ethical questions that is characteristic" of the Elizabethan-Jacobean period, focussing on the "artistic equation of honour with reputation"; refers to Women Beware Women.

157 Akrigg, G.P.V. "Middleton: An Allusion to the Shakspere First Folio?" SAB 21 (1946): 25-6. Refers to the verses to Webster's Duchess of Malfi, written by Middleton in 1623, the same year as the First Folio.

158 Anderson, Donald K. "The Banquet of Love in English Drama (1595-1642)." JEGP 63 (1964): 422-32. Discusses the love-feast as a preliminary to lovemaking or seduction, with reference to Women Beware Women and The Bloody Banquet (which has been attributed to Middleton at times), among others.

159 Andrews, Michael C. "'Sweetness' in The Changeling." YES 1 (1971): 63-67. Suggests that "sweet" may be "a sexual metaphor as well as an abstract term of approbation or endearment," in a development of the food image.

160 Bains, Y.S. "Middleton's Blurt, Master Constable as a Burlesque on Love." In Essays Presented to Amy G. Stock, Professor of English, Rajasthan University, 1961-65. ed. R.K. Kaul. Jaipur, 1965. Pp. 41-57. (**New Cambridge Bibliography and Popular School)

161 Baker, Donald C. "Metaphors in Swift's A Tale of a Tub and Middleton's The Family of Love." NQ 203 (1958): 107-8. A discussion of the "philosophy of clothes" and "the Aeolist myth" in Tale of a Tub sections II and VIII and Family of Love IV.i; notes that the example in Family is "the only instance of both the satirical devices being employed together, or even by the same author, until Swift."

162 Balch, Marston. "Thomas Middleton: Three Hundred Years After." Theatre Arts Monthly 11 (1927): 911-16. A general survey of Middleton's work, and his reputation as of the early years of this century; notes that Middleton's "realism" makes his plays incapable of being revived, with the exception perhaps of The Changeling.

163 Balch, Marston Stevens. "Christopher Bullock and The Mayor of Queenborough." In Jacobean Miscellany 2. Salzburg, 1981. Pp. 3-46. Discusses the content and author of the 1710 production of the Mayor as a "one-act farce." Uses possible parallels between this borrowing and Bullock's treatment of The Slip (from A Mad World, My Masters) to identify Bullock as the author of the farce and the 1710 Mayor as originally Middleton's play.

164 ----------. "Contemporary Imitators ["Imitations" on title page] of Thomas Middleton." In Jacobean Miscellany 2. Salzburg, 1981. Pp. 47-79. A discussion of Middleton's influence on younger playwrights, especially Fletcher and Rowley, and a number of others, from Armin to Shirley.

165 ----------. "Some Middleton Revivals." In Jacobean Drama Studies No. 95. Salzburg, 1980. Pp. 34-75. A review of the early Restoration revivals and adaptations of a number of Middleton's plays.

166 Bald, R.C. "Assembled Texts." Library (series 4) 12 (1931): 243-48. A defence of his edition of A Game at Chess (see review by Dover Wilson, 606); discusses texts "assembled" from different sources.

167 ----------. "The Chronology of Middleton's Plays." MLR 32 (1937): 33-43. Discusses and establishes with some authority the chronology of Middleton's work (not just plays); offers as well the alternative suggestions of others. Except for a few later changes, the generally accepted chronology.

168 ----------. "An Early Version of Middleton's Game at Chesse." MLR 38 (1943): 177-80. Discusses the discovery of a sixth manuscript of Game at Chess, which appears to be in the hand of Ralph Crane, with corrections possibly by Middleton himself. Notes that this version, as well as stating explicitly the chessboard configuration of the opening scene, omits the Fat Bishop and his pawn, and is therefore probably the earliest version of the play to survive; suggests that the satire on Spalatro was an "afterthought" by Middleton, possibly to add a part for Rowley.

169 ----------. "The Foul Papers of a Revision." Library (series 4) 26 (1945): 37-50. A discussion of the 1608 edition of Your Five Gallants; suggests that the basis of the edition was the author's own "foul papers" with authorial revisions included. Gives other examples of the same type of "unsatisfactory" text, also based on foul papers.

170 ----------. "A Game at Chesse." TLS 17 May 1928: 379. Rejects the "allegory of the Palatinate" suggestion and the suggestion of Buckingham's sponsorship; suggests August for play's performance, as the King was by then out of London. (A response to Wright, 572.)

171 ----------. "Middleton's Civic Employments." MP 31 (1933): 65-78. Lists and gives details about the various entertainments Middleton wrote for the City of London, with a chronology as well.

172 ----------. "A New Manuscript of Middleton's Game at Chesse." MLR 25 (1930): 474-78. Describes the condition of a new manuscript (the fifth, in 1928) that is the "worst" and probably the latest to survive. Notes the many variants and corruptions, the "work of a careless scribe," and concludes that the manuscript was possibly transcribed from "two transcripts by the scribe responsible for the source of the text of quarto I." (For an argument with much of Bald's Game at Chess manuscript conclusions, see Zimmerman, 576.)

173 ----------. "The Sources of Middleton's City Comedies." JEGP 33 (1934): 373-87. Describes how Middleton made use of "ideas and situations that were common at the time," in pamphlets, stage conventions, and contemporary drama, with particular discussion of the sources of Michaelmas Term, A Chaste Maid in Cheapside and Your Five Gallants.

174 Barber, Charles. "A Rare Use of the Word 'Honour' as a Criterion of Middleton's Authorship." Essays and Studies 38 (1957): 161-8. Notes Middleton's use of the word "honour" as "a bow, curtsey, obeisance"--of only twelve uses of this kind in 127 plays, eight are in plays by Middleton. (See further his book, 005.)

175 Barker, Richard H. "The Authorship of The Second Maiden's Tragedy and The Revenger's Tragedy." SAB 20 (1945): 51-62 and 121-133. Reviews the evidence for Middleton's authorship of both plays; decides on stylistic and thematic grounds that both are in all probability by Middleton.

176 Batchelor, J.B. "The Pattern of Women Beware Women." YES 2 (1972): 78-88. Relates Middleton's version of the plot to the sources; discusses how the changes he made fit the "retribution" theme of the play. Explains the emblematic significance of the concluding deaths.

177 Bawcutt, N.W. "The Changeling: A Source for the Subplot." NQ 200 (1955): 233. Notes the similarities between The Family of Love and Changeling's subplot; argues that this indicates Middleton's influence in the "Rowley" subplot (although Family of Love is not without authorship controversy; see Lake, 147).

178 ----------. "Middleton's The Phoenix as a Royal Play." NQ 201 (1956): 287-88. Establishes that Phoenix was given royal performance on 20 Feb. 1603/4 and was therefore the first royal play of the reign of James I, "Middleton's offering to James I." Discusses the example the play gives of the training of a prince. Part of a NQ discussion; see Power (466 and 467) and Dodson (238) for the second and third parts of the examination.

179 Beck, Ervin. "Terence Improved: The Paradigm of the Prodigal Son in English Renaissance Drama." RenD (n.s.) 6 (1973): 107-22. A study of the "ubiquitous" prodigal son plot, giving its literary history and emphasising the son-father elements of the essential "archetype"--it is "not that he is a prodigal, but that he is a son who denies or misvalues his heritage and has to learn through experience to appreciate it" that is the vital element. Contrasts the "prodigal son play" with Roman New Comedy; discusses A Trick to Catch the Old One, A Mad World, My Masters, and Michaelmas Term

180 Berger, Thomas L. "Further Notes on the Text of Blurt Master-Constable." ELN 13 (1975): 90-98. A development of Janzen's article (see 334); gives notes on "at least ten other cruxes" in the text of the play's 1602 quarto.

181 ----------. "The Petrarchan Fortress of The Changeling." RenP 1969: 37-46. Discusses the use in both plots of an equivalence between the "fortress" and the "lady," a conceit used by Petrarch.

182 Bergeron, David M. "Middleton's Moral Landscape: A Chaste Maid in Cheapside and The Triumphs of Truth." In "Accompaninge the players," pp. 133-146. A discussion of Middleton's "thoroughly middle-class values and concerns" in his two works of circa 1613, his "finest comedy" and his "richest Lord Mayor's Show." Notes the contrasting themes of "sin and corruption" in the play and "virtue" in the pageant and makes connections in setting, imagery and theme between the two works, including the "Seven Deadly Sins" pattern evident in both. In both works, he concludes, Middleton "assays the moral landscape of London."

183 Berggren, Paula S. "'A Prodigious Thing': The Jacobean Heroine in Male Disguise." PQ 62 (1983): 383-402. A discussion of "Elizabethan transvestite heroines"; discusses Middleton pp. 389-93. Finds that "generally, Middleton puts women into men's clothes to signal toughness or sexual indiscretion." Discusses The Roaring Girl, No Wit No Help, More Dissemblers Besides Women, and, extensively, The Widow.

184 ----------. "'Womanish' Mankind" Four Jacobean Heroines." International Journal of Women's Studies 1 (1978): 349-63. Argues that "in an era when human potential seemed thwarted," women made ideal heroines, being "thralls to a social system that practiced the patriarchal repression the Stuarts tried to restore," and yet capable of "areas of human sensitivity and capacities for resilience" not shown by male characters. Discusses the ways in which Middleton's heroines are portrayed sympathetically as "young women trying to expand their domestic rights" against "domineering parent figures"; discusses Beatrice ("intellectually limited and physically grasping") and Bianca, whose character "fosters a belief in the human soul."

185 Berlin, Normand. "The 'Finger' Image and Relationship of Character in The Changeling." English Studies in Africa 12 (1969): 162-66. An analysis of the "finger-ring-hand-glove" group of images; finds it part of sexual and psychological imagery used in the development of the relationship between Beatrice and De Flores--"the image is dropped when De Flores and Beatrice become one" in "the spiritual partnership that has ... led to hell."

186 Berry, Francis. "Pronouns in The Revenger's Tragedy." In his Poets' Grammar: Person, Time and Mood in Poetry. London: Routledge and Kegan Paul, 1958. Pp. 80-86. Mentions his "intuitive belief" that The Revenger's Tragedy and The Atheist's Tragedy have the same author; notes "Tourneur"'s distinction between "thou" and "you" and suggests this as a possible authorship proof, were Middleton's usage studied.

187 Bowers, Fredson Thayer. "Middleton's Fair Quarrel and the Duelling Code." JEGP 36 (1937): 40-65. Discusses the multiple meanings of the word "fair" as used in the play; relates the events in the play to Jacobean duelling conventions and concludes that the play censures the degradation of what should be a "lofty possession" (honour) to the "ill-conceived reason for the hasty and ridiculous quarrels" over which Jacobean duels were fought.

188 ----------. "Notes on Running Titles as Bibliographical Evidence." Library (series 4) 19 (1938): 315-38. A discussion of printing techniques; notes that The Roaring Girl was probably printed with one skeleton, but with one running title replaced from time to time; he has "reverse[d] the opinions" he previously (189) held (see McManaway, 420, for the argument that changed his mind).

189 ----------. "Thomas Dekker: Two Textual Notes." Library (series 4) 18 (1937): 338-41. Discusses The Roaring Girl 1611 in the Dyce copy, its variation from other copies, and the relationship between The Honest Whore 1604, The Honest Whore 1605, and The Converted Courtesan.

190 Bowers, R.H. "The Masque of the Four Seasons." NQ 197 (1952): 96-7. Discusses a masque performed for Sir Thomas Myddelton and mentions Middleton's connections with his namesake.

191 Bradbrook, Muriel C. "Lucrece and Othello." TLS 27 Oct. 1950: 677. Notes the similarity of Othello II.ii.177-80 and Middleton's Lucrece sig B5 in the use of chrysolite as an "emblem of unwavering faith"; comments on Shakespeare's apparent borrowing of an image from a poem heavily indebted in its turn to his Lucrece poem.

192 ----------. "The Politics of Pageantry: Social Implications in Jacobean London." In Poetry and Drama 1570-1700: Essays in Honour of Harold F. Brooks, ed. Antony Coleman and Antony Hammond. London: Methuen, 1981. Pp. 60-75. A discussion of the political and religious aspects of mayoral pageants; includes comment on Middleton's 1613 show for Sir Thomas Myddelton and the grocers, "the most strongly Puritan of the companies," his anti-Spanish 1617 pageant, and A Game at Chess.

193 Bradford, Gamaliel. "The Women of Middleton and Webster." Sewanee Review 29 (1921): 14-29. Discusses the "lively comedies of social life and manners" that the two wrote; finds that Middleton has Shakespeare's "comic richness and sweetness." Provides nothing extensive or new about the women characters; leaves out Women Beware Women's Livia.

194 Brittin, Norman A. "Middleton's Style and Other Jacobean Styles: Adjectives and Authorship." In "Accompaninge the players," pp. 39-66. A study of the use of adjectives by Jacobean authors; uses it to support the case for Middleton's authorship of The Revenger's Tragedy (briefly) and to suggest characteristics of the authors considered (Middleton is "realistic, worldly, critical, pessimistic"). Concludes that Jonson's and Middleton's uses of adjectives "attest their distinctiveness and their eminence."

195 Brodsky, G.W.S. "The Changeling: A Possible Narrative Source in The Faerie Queene." NQ 222 (1977): 517-18. Finds similarities to Book III, Canto 10, in plot elements and in the "blindness induced by cupidity."

196 Brodwin, Leonora Leet. "Authorship of The Second Maiden's Tragedy: A Reconsideration of the Manuscript Attribution to Chapman." SP 63 (1966): 51-77. Discusses the manuscript and examines internal evidence for Chapman; finds philosophic and literary parallels with other Chapman plays and a parallel treatment of love and stoicism. Evaluates the evidence for Massinger, Tourneur and Middleton and argues for Chapman as the original author, with Middleton, Marston or Ford possible revisers. (For refutation, see Lancashire, 365.)

197 Bromham, A.A. "The Date of The Witch and the Essex Divorce Case." NQ 225 (1980): 149-152. Discusses Bald's date of 1616 and argues that the witchcraft involved in the Essex divorce was a matter of gossip before the Overbury murder trials of 1615; there were "aspects of the case which were already common knowledge in 1613," when the annulment was granted.

198 ----------. "Middleton's Cardinal of Milan." NQ 225 (1980): 155-57. Discusses the possibility of the Cardinal in More Dissemblers Besides Women (using Lake's date of 1619) being a portrait of the same prelate satirised in A Game at Chess, the Archibishop of Spalatro, who converted to Protestantism and then later recanted.

199 ----------. "Thomas Middleton's Hengist, King of Kent and John Povet's Shorte Treatise of Politike Power." NQ 226 (1982): 143-5. Suggests that the source for the use of the Hengist/Horsa story as a political, anti-Spanish plot, with the Saxons corresponding to the Catholics, is Povet's tract; Povet's book was associated with the Parliamentary opposition some years later, as Middleton may have been (see also Heinemann, 144 and 300).

200 Brooks, John B. "Middleton's Stepfather and the Captain of The Phoenix." NQ 206 (1961): 382-4. Suggests that the Captain was a portrait of Middleton's stepfather Thomas Harvey, Castiza a tribute to his mother and Fidelio possibly a portrait of himself. Argues that Harvey was not only "the basis for a character" but also a cause of "that pessimistic view of human nature which underlies" Middleton's work.

201 Brown, Arthur. "The Play within a Play: An Elizabethan Dramatic Device." E&S (n.s.) 13 (1960): 36-48. A discussion of plays with "another play [inserted] as part of the main action." Comments on Women Beware Women (p. 40; "the play or masque within a play is here no more than a convenience ... [the] denouement is badly handled") and A Mad World, My Masters ("here Middleton has used the device quite satisfactorily"). (Essay is reprinted in Jacobean Theatre, ed. Bernard Harris--see Parker, 453.)

202 Brustein, Robert. "We Are Two Cultural Nations." New Republic 21 Nov. 1964: 25-6, 28. A review of Elia Kazan's New York production of The Changeling that points out the difficulties of producing a Renaissance play in the United States; finds the production dreadful but praises the play: "out of a sequence of Tussaud horrors, Middleton snatches a Petrarchan lyricism." (This article is reprinted in Brustein's collection Seasons of Discontent: Dramatic Opinions 1959-1965 [New York: Simon and Schuster, 1965], pp. 252-59.) See Hewes and McCarten for more reviews of the same production (302 and 415).

203 Bryant, J.A., Jr. "Middleton as a Modern Instance." Sewanee Review 84 (1976): 572-94. Describes Middleton's impersonality and his Calvinistic perspective, with details from A Trick to Catch the Old One, A Chaste Maid in Cheapside and The Changeling; argues that modern audiences "are ready to read Middleton's plays as if Middleton had written them for their own amusement."

204 Buckingham, Elisabeth Lee. "Campion's Art of English Poesie and Middleton's A Chaste Maid in Cheapside." PMLA 43 (1928): 784-92. Finds a parallel between the Allwit situation and Campion's work; suggests that both are based on the same scandal, or possibly Middleton's version on Campion's, dated 1602. Argues as a result for a 1611-14 date for Chaste Maid.

205 Bueler, Lois E. "The Rhetoric of Change in The Changeling." ELR 14 (1984): 95-113. Discusses the language of the play and the way in which this language is itself "the object of change"; concludes that "the audience is expected to notice the rhetorical effects," chief among which is "the sense that the grammatical, semantic, and logical ground is shifting beneath us."

206 Bullock, Helene B. "Thomas Middleton and the Fashion in Playmaking." PMLA 42 (1927): 766-76. Argues that Middleton, "more scientist than artist," simply followed the fashion in his plays and provided a portrait of low life that is "untrue to the whole of human nature." Suggests that the impulse for the romantic comedies came from Rowley, who was the "possessor of a temper ... more noble than Middleton's." (See Symons, 115--this attitude towards Rowley is the "Baconian heresy" of Middleton criticism, which had to be refuted before Middleton could be accepted as the guiding force in The Changeling and, to a lesser degree, A Fair Quarrel.)

207 Bullough, Geoffrey. "The Game at Chesse: How It Struck a Contemporary." MLR 49 (1954): 156-63. Describes a letter that gives an audience member's reaction to the performance of A Game at Chess: he found it "sound" on religion and politics. Also gives a version of the "Verses sent to King James," supposedly sent by Middleton to excuse himself (also a version in Dyce's edition). (See also Tannenbaum, 540, and Wagner's response, 552.)

208 Burelbach, Frederick M., Jr. "Theme and Structure in The Spanish Gipsy." Humanities Association Bulletin 19.2 (1968): 37-41. Discusses the four plots, all "variations on the theme of the prodigal son"; concludes that each ends with the classic repentance and forgiveness of the parable.

209 ----------. "Middleton and Rowley's The Changeling, I.i.52-56." Explicator 26 (1968): item 60. Discusses the "sea-see" pun and its relationship to levels of "knowing."

210 Burke, Harry R. "The Kaleidoscopic Vision: Multiple Perspectives in Middleton's A Chaste Maid in Cheapside." Iowa State Journal of Research 57 (1982): 123-29. Discusses Middleton's manner of presenting multiple perspectives on the characters and themes of Chaste Maid; argues with Williams, 562.

211 Champion, Larry S. "Tragic Vision in Middleton's Women Beware Women." ES 57 (1976): 410-424. Argues that Middleton "projects a broad view of tragedy which indicts not only the single figure but also society at large" and its "pervasive corruption." Finds that sympathy is retained for "Brancha [sic]", Isabella and Leantio, who are not "entirely self-motivated" but are also victims of "social forces." (See his monograph, 024, for more detail on Middleton's "tragic vision.")

212 Charney, Maurice. "Comic Villainy in Shakespeare and Middleton." In his (as editor) Shakespearean Comedy. New York: New York Literary Forum, 1980. Pp. 165-173. Argues that Shakespeare and Middleton had "an understanding of evil that sets them apart from other Elizabethan dramatists"; they muted the "flamboyance of evil" to create "believable and persuasive villains of daily life." Discusses Allwit and Livia ("Iago's true heir") among Middleton's "villains."

213 ----------. "Webster vs. Middleton, or the Shakespearean Yardstick in Jacobean Tragedy." In English Renaissance Drama: Essays in Honour of Madeleine Doran and Mark Eccles, ed. Standish Henning, Robert Kimbrough, and Richard Knowles. Carbondale and Edwardsville: Southern Illinois University Press, 1976. Pp. 118-27. In part, a review of Frost's School of Shakespeare (see 040); a plea for an end to the "Shakespearean yardstick" approach to Jacobean drama, especially in poetry.

214 Chatterji, Ruby. "Dating the Jesuit Ovation Used by Thomas Middleton in A Game At Chess." NQ 222 (1977): 141-2. Places the date at April to June 1623.

215 ----------. "Theme, Imagery, and Unity in A Chaste Maid in Cheapside." RenD 8 (1966): 105-26. Discusses the variety of imagery in the play--family relationships, food, anatomy, word play--and concludes that the play has "unity in variety."

216 ----------. "Unity and Disparity in Michaelmas Term." SEL 8 (1968): 349-63. A study of one of Middleton's "satirical plays on social life with a relatively serious and moralistic outlook." Finds a "bifocal" comic vision, in which the allegorical set pieces and the "realistic" scenes do not quite match, but the overall effect is that of "a satirically depraved world."

217 Christian, Mildred Gayler. "An Autobiographical Note by Thomas Middleton." NQ 175 (1938): 259-60. Notes a reference by Middleton to Queen's College, Oxford, where he matriculated, in his Triumphs of Love and Antiquity.

218 ----------. "Middleton's Acquaintance with the Merrie Conceited Jests of George Peele." PMLA 50 (1935): 753-60. Suggests that the "gentleman-cony-catchers" of Mad World, Your Five Gallants and The Puritan (sometimes attributed to Middleton--see Lake, 147) are based on Peele's stories; uses this to date the composition of the plays at 1607-8, soon after the publication of the Merrie Jests. (Bald, 167, questions this; he notes that the 1607-8 date is the publication date of the three plays, and sees this as Paul's Boys making some money from the popularity of the Jests with the revival of some older--1604-5--plays.) [Non-Dramatic Sources for the Rogues in Middleton's Plays, Christian's dissertation (Baltimore, 1936), of which this article is a part, is frequently cited but has never been published.]

219 ----------. "Middleton's Residence at Oxford." MLN 61 (1946): 90-91. Places Middleton at Oxford April 1598 to at least 28 June 1600 or 12 December 1601. (See Eccles, 251.)

220 ----------. "A Sidelight on the Family History of Thomas Middleton." SP 44 (1947): 490-96. Gives details of the death of Middleton's father, his mother's remarriage, to Thomas Harvey, and Harvey's subsequent career. (See Eccles, 252.)

221 Cohen, Ralph Alan. "The Function of Setting in Eastward Ho." RenP 1973: 85-96. Discusses the audience reaction to the familiar settings in city comedies; makes passing reference to Middleton as one of the authors of "comedies of London life."

222 Cope, Jackson I. "The Date of Middleton's Women Beware Women." MLN 76 (1961): 295-300. Finds parallels between Women Beware Women and The Triumphs of Truth (October 1613); suggests as a result 1613 or 1614 as a date for the play--a much earlier date than is usually accepted (Bald, 167: c.1621), but one that has gained some support. (In part a rejection of Maxwell's evidence for 1621; see Maxwell, 404.)

223 Core, George. "The Canker and the Muse: Imagery in Women Beware Women." RenP 1968: 65-76. Finds a "unified moral vision" in the play; discusses the meanings and various uses of the dominant image, the canker.

224 Covatta, Anthony. "A Marston-Middleton Parallel: New Light on the Growth of City Comedy." NQ 218 (1973): 459-60. Finds several parallels between The Dutch Courtesan (1603-4) and A Mad World, My Masters (1604-6); suggests that if Middleton has borrowed from Marston, then Marston is more important a playwright than has been thought. Observes that "Marston is more compassionate in theory, Middleton in practice" in regards to the punishment each deals out to his courtesan.

225 ----------. "Remarriage in Michaelmas Term." NQ 217 (1972): 460-61. Notes that Thomasine is returned to Quomodo at the end of the play--a response to some doubt about this. Comments further that the "return of Thomasine to Quomodo, her legal but imperfect husband, parallels the return of the Essex estate to Easy, its rightful but inexperienced owner."

226 Craig, Hardin. "Textual Degeneration of Elizabethan and Stuart Plays: An Examination of Plays in Manuscript." Revue International de Philosophie 46 (1960): 71-84. (**Popular School)

227 Craik, T.W. "Notes on the Text of Three Passages in The Changeling." NQ 222 (1977): 120-22. Notes on III.iii.187-98, V.i.96-102, and V.iii.87-94. These emendations are continued in "Further Proposed Emendations in The Changeling," NQ 225 (1980): 324-327.

228 ----------. "The Revenger's Tragedy." EIC 6 (1956): 482-85. Notes that revengers are always caught in the end, as a convention of the revenge play and not necessarily as a moral judgement--a response to Peter, 456.

229 Cutts, John P. "The Original Music to Middleton's The Witch." SQ 7 (1956): 203-9. Discusses the various evidence surrounding the link between the Witch songs and the Macbeth songs; notes the existence of the music for the "Come away" song, setting by Robert Johnson, and publishes it, along with the "'witches Dance.'"

230 ----------. "Who Wrote the Hecate-Scene?" Shakespeare Jahrbuch 94 (1958): 200-202. Discusses the attribution of Macbeth III.v to Middleton; concludes that, as the songs in the scene are from Middleton's The Witch and "all available evidence points to" his authorship of them, "Middleton's name cannot safely be dismissed from any consideration of the Hecate scenes in Macbeth." A reply to Flatter, 273; for Flatter's response, see 272. (See also Frost, 040.)

231 ----------. "Jacobean Masque and Stage Music." Music and Letters 35 (1954): 185-200. A revision of Lawrence's description of British Museum additional manuscript 10444 (see 373); notes that Sibley's section of "Lost Masques with Known Titles" (see 103) is now outdated (no allowance made for anti-masques). Lists the contents of MS 10444 and comments on them; notes the "first" and "second" witches' dances and argues that the first is from Middleton's The Witch, while the second must be from Macbeth (only one dance in The Witch).

232 ----------. "Robert Jonson: King's Musician in His Majesty's Public Entertainment." Music and Letters 36 (1955): 110-125. Discusses Johnson's musical settings, including two songs from The Witch, "Come away ... Heckert" (the one loaned to Macbeth) and "In a maiden time profest."

233 Davidson, Clifford. "Middleton and the Family of Love." English Miscellany 20 (1970): 81-92. Discusses fully the real "Family of Love" sect, "the epitome of non-Catholic religious dissent," and its relationship to Middleton's play The Family of Love. Quotes primary texts in support of his contention that the play is "a propaganda piece which attacks the Sectarian impulse that was felt in those days to pose a serious threat to the ordering of the commonwealth." (See also Ebel, 248.)

234 Davis, Richard A. and Alan R. Young. "'Strange Cunning' in Thomas Middleton's A Game at Chess." Discusses the metaphor of the chess game and its use in Middleton's "typically complex irony."

235 ----------. "The Phoenix: Middleton's Didactic Comedy." PLL 4 (1968): 121-130. Analyses the morality play structure of Phoenix; concludes that the play, unlike Middleton's later plays, offers a pair of truly virtuous characters and thus indicates that Middleton's "view of man is not utterly bleak": we see "corruption through the eyes of the Prince" in Phoenix, whereas in later plays "we see corrupt human nature" for ourselves, but Middleton's moral universe still contains virtue.

236 Dessen, Alan C. "Middleton's The Phoenix and the Allegorical Tradition. SEL 6 (1966): 291-308. Discusses the elements of the morality tradition in the play, and especially its similarities to the "estates" play; it "successfully accomplished the purpose of an 'estates' morality without itself being a morality play," with all the allegorical elements literalised. Concludes that in Phoenix, the "corrupt and diseased society" is countered by various "incorruptible" institutions.

237 Dodson, Daniel B. "Blurt Master Constable." NQ 204 (1959): 61-65. Observes that Blurt is "totally lacking in the mordant bestiality and the cynicism" of Middleton's city comedy; attributes it to Dekker, who excels in "wholesome provincial naivety." (But see Holmes, 145 and 318.)

238 ----------. "King James and The Phoenix -- Again." NQ 203 (1958): 434-37. A discussion of the "political exemplum" elements of the play. Part of a lengthy Notes and Queries discussion; see also Bawcutt (178) and Power (466 and 467) for the first and second parts of the exchange.

239 ----------. "Middleton's Livia." PQ 27 (1948): 376-81. Discusses Women Beware Women's builder of the "edifice of unholy love"; one of the few specific considerations of Livia.

240 Doob, Penelope B.R. "A Reading of The Changeling." ELR 3 (1973): 183-206. Considers the play as much "symbolic morality play" as "naturalistic tragedy"; discusses the emblematic and symbolic elements in the play, and the metaphoric relationship between folly and madness on one hand, and sin and its effects on the other.

241 Dowling, Margaret. "A Note of Moll Cutpurse--'The Roaring Girl.'" RES (n.s.) 10 (1934): 67-71. Describes a reference to a thief-catching done by Moll in 1621.

242 Duffy, Joseph M. "Madhouse Optics: The Changeling." Comparative Drama 8 (1974): 184-198. Discusses the play's central metaphor of the asylum; concludes that Beatrice is tragic in her failure to see until too late that "one may become lost in lunatic spaces of the earth without leaving the world of self." Feels that the play is pessimistic in its final "nightmare of damnation."

243 Dunkel, W.D. "The Authorship of Anything for a Quiet Life." PMLA 43 (1928): 793-9. Finds Quiet Life like Middleton's comedies in its "rampant boisterousness"; concludes that Middleton is the author and Webster merely the reviser. (In part, a response to Sykes--see 538.)

244 ----------. "The Authorship of The Puritan." PMLA 45 (1930): 804-808. Supports the case for Middleton's authorship with similarities to "Middleton's dramatic method."

245 ----------. "The Authorship of The Revenger's Tragedy." PMLA 46 (1931): 781-85. Argues for Middleton's authorship with similarities to others of Middleton's plays and suggests Revenger's Tragedy's identity with Middleton's "lost" The Viper and Her Brood (see Hillebrand, 305).

246 ----------. "Did Not Rowley Merely Revise Middleton?" PMLA 48 (1933): 799-805. A suggestion about the authorship collaboration of Middleton and Rowley; discusses Spanish Gipsy especially. A rather famous article, to whose title several critics have responded (both "yes" and "no").

247 Dunlap, Rhodes. "James I, Bacon, Middleton, and the Making of *The Peacemaker*." *Holzknecht*, pp. 82-94. Discusses the authorship and origin of the pamphlet entitled *The Peacemaker* (1618). Demonstrates that James I knew and approved of the pamphlet and aided Middleton in its distribution, encouraging Middleton in his arguments against duelling and for "the blessings of peace." Notes as well Middleton's borrowings from Bacon in a few passages.

248 Ebel, Julia G. "The Family of Love: Sources of Its History in England." *Huntingdon Library Quarterly* 30 (1967): 331-43. A survey of material on the original "Family of Love," the "transitional stage" between evangelical Anabaptists and Quakers. Notes that references to "Familism" are not always specific--it became "a generalized term of abuse." (For another point of view see Davidson, 233.)

249 Eberle, Gerald J. "The Composition and Printing of Middleton's *A Mad World, My Masters*." *Studies in Bibliography* 3 (1930): 246-52. A detailed discussion of possible printing methods used; suggests two different compositors.

250 ----------. "Dekker's Part in *The Family of Love*." In *Joseph Quincy Adams Memorial Studies*, pp. 723-38. Discusses, scene by scene, the possible contributions of Dekker to *Family of Love*; concludes that it is "a revision by Dekker and Middleton of an early play written by Middleton with considerable help from Dekker."

251 Eccles, Mark. "Middleton's Birth and Education." *RES* (n.s.) 7 (1931): 431-41. This study of the information available about Middleton's christening and education led to the acceptance of a later (1580 rather than 1570) birthdate for Middleton and the subsequent revision of his biography (see following entry). This article notes how the dates given enable a reevaluation of Middleton's early work, previously thought incomprehensibly dull but now understood as the work of a young writer. Attributes *The Puritan* to Middleton.

252 ----------. "Thomas Middleton a Poett." *SP* 54 (1957): 516-36. This important survey of the various sources of information about Middleton's life and the chronology of his early works completed Eccles' revision of the traditional Middleton biography and helped initiate a complete change in critical attitudes towards Middleton's early non-dramatic works.

253 Ekeblad, Inga-Stina. "An Approach to Tourneur's Imagery." MLR 54 (1959): 489-98. A reaction to the famous Ellis-Fermor and Mincoff studies of the imagery (each came to a different conclusion about authorship; see individual entries). Examines "the function of imagery as part of dramatic structure and technique" in order to demonstrate the similarity of Revenger's and Atheist's Tragedy; concludes that there is "a firm integration, a unity of aim, of the imagery with the dramatic structure and technique" in both plays.

254 ----------. "A Note on The Revenger's Tragedy." NQ 200 (1955): 98-99. Argues aginst Middleton's authorship; notes reasons for assigning Revenger's Tragedy to the Globe, and not to the Children at the private theatres, as are all "Middleton's extant plays known to have been written by 1608," including the lost Viper and Her Brood (therefore Revenger's is not Viper).

255 ----------. "On the Authorship of The Revenger's Tragedy." English Studies 41 (1960): 225-40 (written in 1956). Refutes the attribution of the play to Middleton through a discussion of the components of The Revenger's Tragedy. Comments that it contains a "moral allegory," while Middleton's comedies concentrate on "comic effect" and his tragedies on "psychological re-creation of characters' minds"; in neither case is there the "emphatic communication of moral truth" that she sees in Revenger's Tragedy.

256 ----------, as Inga-Stina Ewbank. "Realism and Morality in Women Beware Women." E&S 22 (1969): 57-70. A discussion of the morality of Women Beware Women, concluding that it lies in Middleton's particular vision that sees "the horror of life ... in what men will do to men (or women to women)."

257 ----------. "The Tenant of Wildfell Hall and Women Beware Women." NQ 208 (1963): 449-50. Notes the similarity of Tenant's chess game to Women Beware Women; traces Anne Bronte's possible access to the 1657 edition of Women.

258 ----------, as Inga-Stina Ewbank. "'These Pretty Devices': A Study of Masques in Play." In A Book of Masques in Honour of Allardyce Nicoll, ed. T.J.B. Spencer and Stanley Wells. Cambridge: Cambridge University Press, 1967. Pp. 405-448. A discussion of the various ways in which masques are inserted and used in Elizabethan-Jacobean plays, and how they are "very often central in the structure of the play where they occur." Discusses the unmasking masque of Your Five Gallants's denouement and also the masking in Revenger's Tragedy, and in Women Beware Women, where the final masque is "an exhibition of ironic retribution."

The collection is reviewed by G.R. Hibbard in NQ 213 (1968): 273-74. He finds the work a good introduction to masques, a useful history of the form, and a valuable presentation of material not easily accessible to the general student, and laments the lack of an index. For another selection that concerns Middleton, see Bald, 637.

Another review, by Peter Ure in MLR 64 (1969): 140-41, hails the collection as "absolutely worthwhile" and "indispensable", although the reviewer has some minor queries.

259 ----------. "A Textual Note on The Changeling." NQ 200 (1955): 156-7. Notes an error in the Havelock Ellis (Old Mermaid) edition of the play, in V.iii.152-6 ("I that am of your blood" should be "I am that of your blood"--a correction made in more recent editions).

260 [Eliot, T.S.] "Tourneur and The Revenger's Tragedy." TLS 1 Jan. 1931: 12. Restates Eliot's position on the authorship question--he favours Tourneur over Middleton. A response to Oliphant (see 446; for Oliphant's answer to this article, see 448); Eliot's original essay on Tourneur, a review of the Nicoll edition of Tourneur's plays, appeared in TLS for November 13, 1930, and is reprinted in Selected Essays (see 032).

261 Ellis-Fermor, Una M. "The Imagery of The Revengers Tragedie and The Atheists Tragedie." MLR 30 (1935): 289-301. One of the two famous studies (see Mincoff, 423, for the other one) that analysed Tourneur's imagery using Caroline Spurgeon's statistical method. Compares imagery using categories to build up a description of the playwright who designed the image patterns; concludes that the two plays show a single author, allowing that they are "plays with an interval of some years between them", with Revenger's earlier.

262 Engleberg, Edward. "A Middleton-Rowley Dispute." NQ 198 (1953): 330-332. Suggests that The Changeling III.iv and A Fair Quarrel III.ii show Middleton's attitude towards women and sin, and therefore his hand in these scenes usually given to Rowley.

263 ----------. "Tragic Blindness in The Changeling and Women Beware Women." MLQ 23 (1962): 20-28. Discusses the images of sight in Changeling and points out their counterparts in Women Beware Women. Concludes that Middleton's plays have no large tragic dimension because he "opposes no real clarity of sight to blindness, no rational and ordered universe to offset the optical illusions of his blinded characters."

264 Esselin, Martin. "The Changeling." Plays and Players 26.2 (Nov. 1979): 16-17. A review of the Riverside Studio production; notes the production's use of the "imposter" meaning of changeling throughout and emphasises the play's psychological insight. Finds the production overall "clean, clear and deeply satisfying." (For more discussion of this and the other 1979 London production, see Scott, 100.)

265 Falk, Signi. "Plautus' Persa and Middleton's A Trick to Catch the Old One." MLN 66 (1951): 19-21. Compares plot structures and themes in the two plays and finds many similarities; mentions other Jacobean comedies with similar plots.

266 Fallon, Padriac. "The Unique Genius." The Dublin Magazine 12.3 (1937): 62-69. Finds "the mind" behind The Revenger's Tragedy and The Atheist's Tragedy "one and the same"; sees Tourneur as neurotic.

267 Farnham, William. "The Medieval Comic Spirit in the English Renaissance." Joseph Quincy Adams Memorial Studies, pp. 429-37. Discusses the influence of the medieval comic elements, including the Vice, on Renaissance comedy; mentions Jonson and his contemporaries as inheritors of medieval ideas about folly, vice, and the grotesque.

268 Farr, Dorothy M. "The Changeling." MLR 62 (1967): 586-97. A discussion of the play, concentrating on Middleton's "observant" depiction of ordinary people who are victims of "their capacity for evasion and self-delusion." Developed further in her monograph (141); she assumes Women Beware Women is a later play.

269 Feldman, A. Bronson. "The Yellow Malady: Short Studies of Five Tragedies of Jealousy." Literature and Psychology 6 (1956): 38-52. Discussion includes Women Beware Women; finds Middleton a "merry writer" who "cared as little for art as he cared for morality."

270 Fisher, Margery. "'Bronstrops': A Note on A Faire Quarrel." MLR 35 (1940): 59-62. A study of the derivation and connotation of the word "bronstrops" as used in A Fair Quarrel and other contemporary sources.

271 ----------. "Notes on the Sources of Some Incidents in Middleton's London Plays." RES 15 (1939): 283-93. Middleton's possible use of "talk of the town" incidents is discussed.

272 Flatter, Richard. "Hecate, 'The Other Three Witches,' and Their Songs." Shakespeare Jahrbuch 95 (1959): 225-37. (A response to Cutts, 230; Flatter's initial article follows this one.) Discusses Macbeth IV.i and the witches' dance, with regard to stage directions and the number of witches indicated (concludes that only three are there). Argues that "Come away" and "Black spirits" are not complete songs but only repeated chants, using only the words in the Macbeth text, that may have been later elaborated into songs by Middleton; there is therefore, he concludes, no evidence for Middleton's influence in Macbeth at all. (The argument continues, however; see Frost, 040, for a recent summation.)

273 ----------. "Who Wrote the Hecate-Scene?" Shakespeare Jahrbuch 93 (1957): 196-210. Discusses the attribution of Macbeth III.v to Middleton; refutes this and states Shakespeare's claim to the scene on thematic and plot grounds--"the Hecate-scene is in fact the central scene of the play." For the other side, see Cutts's answer to this article, 230; see also Flatter's response to Cutts's answer.

274 Foakes, R.A. "On the Authorship of The Revenger's Tragedy." MLR 48 (1953): 129-38. Discusses the attribution of the play; finds the stylistic evidence for Middleton's authorship not persuasive. Rejects as well certain internal elements (including versification) used for the Middleton attribution; finds the similarities between the play and The Atheist's Tragedy enough to maintain the Tourneur attribution. (In his edition of the play [London: Methuen, 1966] he moderates his view slightly.)

275 Forker, Charles R. "Shakespearean Imitation in Act 5 of Anything for a Quiet Life." PLL 7 (1970): 75-80. Finds some echoes of I Henry IV in Quiet Life; notes also some similarities to King Lear and The Taming of the Shrew. An amendment to Frost, 040.

276 Foster, Verna Ann. "The Deed's Creature: The Tragedy of Bianca in Women Beware Women." JEGP 78 (1979): 508-21. A sympathetic study of Bianca, one of Middleton's "psychologically convincing characters", with reference to the 1969 Royal Shakespeare Company production and Bianca's effect on an audience. Argues that Bianca's fall results from a need for "protection and emotional security" and her tragedy is that, although she becomes insightful and mature after her seduction, "all her accomplishments are tainted by her first sin."

277 Friedenreich, Kenneth. "How to Read Middleton." The introduction to his (as editor) "Accompaninge the players," pp. 1-14. A discussion of The Widow and its representation of Middleton's art and his "moral field" with its "moral compromise."

278 Fuzier, Jean and Jean-Marie Maguin. "Archetypal Patterns of Honor and Cruelty in Elizabethan Revenger Tragedy." Cahiers Elisabethains 19 (April 1981): 9-25. Discusses archetypal patterns (incest, parenticide and cannibalism) in revenge tragedy; includes discussion of The Revenger's Tragedy, Women Beware Women and The Witch.

279 Gallenca, Christiane. "Baroque Sensibility in The Changeling." Cahiers Elisabethains 25 (April 1984): 73-84. Notes that the play is "characterized by movement and metamorphosis"; argues that the combination of imagery based on the Fall (happiness, temptation, sin, exile) with Greek myth is "typical baroque daring". Concludes that the "mythical residues" multiply "the angles of vision" in the play.

280 Gardner, Helen. "The Changeling and the Tragedy of Damnation." In Shakespeare's Contemporaries, pp. 363-367. Emphasises the change in Beatrice, "the absolute contrast at the beginning and the identity at the close of Beatrice-Joanna and De Flores." (This is a section of the essay; the full essay is reprinted, as "The Tragedy of Damnation," in Elizabethan Drama, pp. 320-341, and was originally published as "Milton's 'Satan' and the Theme of Damnation in Elizabethan Tragedy," in E&S 1 (1948): 46-66.)

281 George, David. "The Problem of Middleton's *The Witch* and its Sources." *NQ* 212 (1967): 209-11. Suggests alternate sources for the witchcraft scenes, *The Atheist's Tragedy* and Virgil rather than the Essex-Overbury murder trial; sets the date therefore at 1614, using the date of *The Atheist's Tragedy* and some suggestions about *The Witch's* possible stage history.

282 ----------. "Thomas Middleton at Oxford." *MLR* 65 (1970): 734-6. Reviews the evidence for Middleton's stay at Oxford; suggests his activities and the origins of his poem "The Ghost of Lucrece."

283 ----------. "Thomas Middleton's Sources: A Survey." *NQ* 216 (1971): 17-24. The summary of George's extensive survey of Middleton's sources; concludes that "given a story line, Thomas Middleton made use of his own observation and his own peculiar psychology to make a play. Now and again, the results of this method are surprisingly fine."

284 ----------. "Some Later Uses of Middleton's *No Wit No Help*." NQ 219 (1974): 290-92. Discusses a ballad that seems to be a descendant (or even, in an earlier form, a source) of *No Wit No Help*'s main plot; notes also Goldsmith's possible use of the subplot of the play for *The Good Natur'd Man*.

285 ----------. "Weather-wise's Almanac and the Date of Middleton's *No Wit, No Help like a Woman's*." *NQ* 211 (1966): 297-301. Uses the Almanac to date the play to the summer of 1611; suggests early 1611/12 as the date of performance. Refers to the epilogue to suggest that the play was an outdoor one, and therefore possibly a Swan play (like *Chaste Maid*).

286 Gilbert, Allan H. "The Prosperous Wittol in Giovanni Battista Modio and Thomas Middleton." *SP* 41 (1944), 235-7. Suggests an Italian source for Allwit in *A Chaste Maid in Cheapside*; "the soliloquy has the air of something borrowed and only partly assimilated."

287 Gill, Roma. "The World of Thomas Middleton." In "*Accompaninge the players*," pp. 15-38. Emphasises Middleton's London locality in his early work (tracts, poems, and comedies) and the development of his irony: he is "totally detached" by *A Chaste Maid in Cheapside*, depicting the world of the "spiritually blind" and the "comfort-seeking (like Bianca in *Women Beware Women*). A general guide to Middleton's art.

288 Golding, M.R. "Variations in the Use of the Masque in English Revenge Tragedy." YES 3 (1973): 44-54. An examination of the use of the masque as "a revenger murder machine"; includes a study of The Revenger's Tragedy and Women Beware Women. Finds that in the latter play, the masque is "a highly formalized and complete example" that brings together "the two major themes of revenge, retribution for seduction and murder"; in this masque, "complication and irony reach their height."

289 Gordon, D.J. "Middleton's No Wit, No Help Like a Woman's and Della Porta's La Sorella." RES (o.s.) 17 (1941): 400-14. Discusses the Sir Oliver Twilight plot and notes its derivation from La Sorella, a "sentimental Italian comedy of the end of the sixteenth century." Points out that the title of No Wit belongs to the main plot and Mrs. Lowwater.

290 Greg, W.W. "Some Notes on Crane's Manuscript of The Witch." Library (series 4) 22 (1942): 208-222. A collation of Reed's edition of 1778 and the manuscript, with a description of Dyce and Bullen's text of the play. Makes some comments on Crane's scribal habits, including his use of parentheses, hyphens and apostrophes.

291 Gross, Alan Gerald. "Middleton's Your Five Gallants: The Fifth Act." PQ 44 (1965): 124-9. Argues that the Boy's speech in V.i was meant to be all in Latin, but is also paraphrased later by Fitsgrave. Deduces that the play was written for an audience that would understand Latin (a private theatre one), and also for one that would not.

292 Hallahan, Huston D. "The Thematic Juxtaposition of the Representational and the Sensational in Middleton's Women Beware Women." Studies in Iconography 2 (1976): 66-84. (**Popular School Update)

293 Hallett, Charles A. "Middleton's Allwit: The Urban Cynic." MLQ 30 (1969): 498-507. Introduces Hallett's thesis that Middleton was "probing through his career into the nature of cynicism." Discusses Allwit as "a study of mediocrity ... the new urban man, who believes in nothing beyond himself," and who is "touched by the naivete of those trusting souls who still believe that there are virtuous people in the world." For Hallett's complete study of Middleton's cynics and his psychological development, see his monograph, 143.

294 ----------. "Middleton's Overreachers and the Ironic Ending." *Tennessee Studies in Literature* 16 (1971): 1-13. A summary of Hallett's arguments about Middleton's overreachers and cynics: his overreachers are "little men who, thinking they are titans, stumble." Argues that the endings of the comedies don't work; "they invariably reflect the moral vision of the author more than they stem from the actions of the characters"; introduces his thesis that Middleton's insight deepens in his later comedy and tragedy. See his monograph, 143.

295 ----------. "Penitent Brothel, the Succubus and Parson's *Resolution*: a Reappraisal of Penitent's Position in Middleton's Canon." *SP* 69 (1972), 72-86. Discusses in detail the stages of Penitent's repentance, taking the passages as Middleton's representation of "a serious and honest repentance." Finds that Penitent marks "the transition point between the satirical comedy of *Michaelmas Term* and the psychological drama of *Women Beware Women* and *The Changeling*." See his monograph, 143.

296 ----------. "The Psychological Drama of *Women Beware Women*." *SEL* 12 (1972): 375-89. Discusses Bianca as a study of growing cynicism; argues that she is not tragic because tragedy implies final recognition and the cynic "confronts every experience by denying responsibility." Introduces the subject of Hallett's later monograph (143): "cynicism is a *moral* disease."

297 ----------. "*Volpone* as the Source of the Sickroom Scene in Middleton's *Mad World*." *NQ* 216 (1971): 24-5. Notes the similarities between Frank Gullman's feigned sickbed and Volpone's feigned death-bed. Dates *Mad World*, therefore, in the later part of 1605, probably after July.

298 Happe, Peter. "The Vice: A Checklist and An Annotated Bibliography." *Research Opportunities in Renaissance Drama* 22 (1979): 17-35. (***Popular School* Update)

299 Hebert, Catherine A. "A Note on the Significance of the Title of Middleton's *The Changeling*." *College Language Association Journal* 12 (1968): 66-69. Discusses the meaning of "changeling" as "one who changes"; finds Beatrice the central "changeling," who is "transformed from a proud amoral girl to a perverted, degraded woman." Discusses as well the other changelings in Alsemero's list in V.iii.

300 Heinemann, Margot. "Middleton's A Game at Chess: Parliamentary-Puritans and Opposition Drama." ELR 5 (1975): 232-50. A discussion of the political implications of the play and of the Parliamentary-Puritan party, anti-Catholic and anti-Spanish, that apparently supported Middleton and Game at Chess. Rejects the view that the play had as its patron Buckingham (for a defence of this, see Moore, 426); suggests instead that the patron may have been Pembroke, who, as Lord Chamberlain, was "the senior officer responsible for the control of the drama" and afterwards apparently "interceded with the King on their behalf." (See also her monograph, 144.)

301 Helton, Tinsley. "Middleton and Rowley's The Changeling, V, iii, 175-77." Explicator 21 (1963): 74. Discusses the meaning of the word "token" in this scene; revises the punctuation in the lines given. (For another view, see Kehler, 340.)

302 Hewes, Henry. "The Teenageling." Saturday Review 21 Nov. 1964: 35. A review of Elia Kazan's The Changeling, New York, 1964. Discusses the methods used to find modernity in the play, the poor central performance, and the language problems with an American cast. (For more reviews of this infamous production, see Brustein, 202, and McCarten, 415.)

303 Hibbard, G.R. "Love, Marriage and Money in Shakespeare's Theatre and Shakespeare's England." In The Elizabethan Theatre VI (1975; see 052), pp. 134-55. Discusses actual marriage routines in Elizabethan England, and odd marriages (including Raleigh's) that gave rise to scandals. Argues that Middleton dramatised Elizabethan marriage "as it was"; suggests that Middleton gave "factual detail" while Shakespeare saw "love as an absolute value."

304 ----------. "The Tragedies of Thomas Middleton and the Decadence of Drama." University of Nottingham Renaissance and Modern Studies 1 (1957): 35-64. Argues that Middleton, in his tragedies, was catering to a decadent public's taste for sensational entertainment; finds that although the impression in these plays of the "hell within" is powerful, the plays are weakened by their endings.

305 Hillebrand, Harold N. "Thomas Middleton's The Viper's Brood." MLN 42 (1927): 35-8. Discusses references to a lawsuit over the play (one no longer extant); uses the information to date the play and make additional biographical suggestions about Middleton.

306 Hogg, James. "John Leanerd's The Rambling Justice or The Jealous Husbands: A Restoration Plagiarism of Thomas Middleton's More Dissemblers Besides Women?" In Elizabethan and Renaissance Studies 70. Salzburg, 1978. Pp. 111-124. An extensive stage history of More Dissemblers, with a summary of the main critical comments; concludes that Leanerd "brazenly incorporated" sections of More Dissemblers, as well as borrowing extensively from Middleton's other work.

307 ----------. "The Spanish Gipsy and Francis Manning's All For the Better, or The Infallible Cure." In Elizabethan and Renaissance Studies 71 (English Miscellany 2). Salzburg, 1978. Pp. 93-134. An exhaustive discussion of Spanish Gipsy's authorship that includes unpublished material, editions, and critical works on Ford; agrees with Lake and others that Gipsy is the work of Dekker and Ford. Gives a stage history of the play and its rebirth as Manning's play, with an extensive discussion of parallels.

308 ----------. "William Hayley's Marcella and Thomas Middleton and William Rowley's The Changeling: A Case of Literary Plagiarism?" In Essays in Honour of Professor Tyrus Hillway, ed. Erwin A. Sturzl. Salzburg, 1977. Pp. 74-128. Gives a stage history of Changeling to the eighteenth century; concludes that Hayley's play was definitely based on Middleton's and represents the only survival of Changeling into the eighteenth century. (See also Balch's monographs on Middleton revivals, 133-136.)

309 Holdsworth, R.V. "A Chaste Maid in Cheapside V.ii.49-50." NQ 222 (1977): 136. A discussion of textual detail in the line given.

310 ----------. "'A Clean Sheet.'" NQ 222 (1977): 205. Notes the figurative use of "clean sheet" in A Fair Quarrel V.i.29, a much earlier date than that given by the O.E.D.

311 ----------. "'Lie By It' in Middleton." NQ 226 (1981): 242. Notes the use of "lie by it" to mean to lie in prison in The Phoenix and The Puritan and possibly The Changeling.

312 ----------. "The Medical Jargon in A Fair Quarrel." RES (n.s.) 23 (1972): 448-54. Discusses the available manuscripts of the play and determines the authoritative one; identifies the source of the medical terminology in the play.

313 ----------. "Michaelmas Term V.i.64-73." Explicator 35 (1976): 13-14 [note: page numbers; The Explicator changed from using item numbers with this volume]. Argues with Levin's gloss of "admit" for "owe" in line 70 (for Levin's edition, see 612); suggests that "possess" is more appropriate, further emphasising the irony of Quomodo's "self-ignorance."

314 ----------. "Middleton and Rowley's A Fair Quarrel: an unnoticed borrowing." NQ 216 (1971): 25-7. Finds resemblances between the main plot and the Sir Walter plot in Chaste Maid; argues that this "furnishes additional proof ... [that] Middleton was responsible for the main plot."

315 ----------. "The Revenger's Tragedy, Ben Jonson, and The Devil's Law Case." RES (n.s.) 31 (1980): 305-10. Discusses Jonson's borrowing from Revenger's Tragedy in The Devil is an Ass (of a passage probably from Middleton's Father Hubbard's Tales) and argues from this for Middleton's authorship of Revenger's. Also mentions other possible borrowings by Jonson from Revenger's, perhaps made when it and Volpone were performed together by the King's Men in 1605-6.

316 ----------. "Two Proverbs in Middleton and Some Contemporaries." NQ 226 (1981): 172-3. Explains "Apollo's smile" in A Fair Quarrel III.ii.95-97 and "sweet meats need sour sauces" in Women Beware Women II.i.196-203 and A Fair Quarrel V.i.308-11 and elsewhere.

317 ----------. "Women Beware Women: An Octavo Reading Vindicated." NQ 223 (1978): 15. A discussion of III.i.77.

318 Holmes, David M. "Thomas Middleton's Blurt, Master-Constable, or The Spaniard's Night-Walk." MLR 64 (1969): 1-10. Defends Middleton's authorship (see also his book on Middleton, 145) on thematic grounds, noting the play's "deliberate juxtaposition of plots," its "disenchanting realism," and its exposure of the world of appearances and "false gentility."

319 ---------- and H[enry] D. Janzen. "A Note on Editing Jacobean Drama." In Editing Seventeenth Century Prose: Papers given at the Convention on Editing Problems, University of Toronto, November 1970, ed. D.I.B. Smith. Tonroto: Hakkert, 1972. Pp. 25-30. A discussion of editing Middleton, with reference to the Dyce edition, Dilke, and more recent editors; argues for the need to recognise Middleton's "derisory tone."

320 Holzknecht, Karl L. "The Dramatic Structure of The Changeling." RenP 1954: 77-87. (Also in Shakespeare's Contemporaries, pp. 367-76.) Discusses the various uses of the word "changeling" in the play, and the various characters to whom it refers. Argues that "Beatrice-Joanna is completely without moral sense, and the play is a study of the deterioration of her character from beauty to deformity."

321 Hoole, William Stanley. "Thomas Middleton's Use of 'Imprese' in Your Five Gallants." SP 31 (1934): 215-23. Discusses Fitsgrave's emblematic devices for the masque and related seventeenth-century uses of emblems; heavily annotated. Of Gallants' devices, he notes that Middleton "seems to have devised for himself those in his play."

322 Horowich, Richard. "Wives, Courtesans, and the Economics of Love in Jacobean City Comedy." CompD 7 (1973): 291-309. Discusses the presentation of love and marriage on the stage; notes that these plays "employ the institution of marriage itself as a testing ground for many of the new economic ideas which were surfacing at the time." Argues that in Middleton, "romantic and idealistic marriages ... are subordinated in intent and importance to the financial trickery and double-dealing"; notes how in Your Five Gallants, A Trick to Catch the Old One, and A Mad World, My Masters, marriage becomes "a marketplace itself."

323 Howards-Hill, T.H. "'Lizards Braine' in Middleton's The Witch." NQ 218 (1973): 458-9. Notes that the Crane manuscript of the play has "Libbards Bane" in the "Black Spirits" song, "libbard" meaning "leopard". Recommends retaining the Crane MS reading.

324 Hoy, Cyrus. "The Shares of Fletcher and his Collaborators in the Beaumont and Fletcher Canon (V)." Studies in Bibliography 13 (1960), 77-108. (Part I, Studies in Bibliography 8 (1956): 129-146, establishes the criteria and gives the table of contractions used for Fletcher.) Part of an extensive series that examines the textual and thematic evidence for authorship in a number of seventeenth-century plays associated in some way with Fletcher, including several of the minor plays in the Middleton canon or apocrypha. Includes specific discussion of Wit at Several Weapons, and The Nice Valor, both of which are attributed to Middleton, with a collaborator (Rowley in Wit; Fletcher in Valor).

325 ----------. "Critical and Aesthetic Problems of Collaboration in Renaissance Drama." Research Opportunities in Renaissance Drama 19 (1976): 3-6. Suggests that authorship studies have now given enough evidence to allow a study of Middleton as a collaborator. (**Popular School Update)

326 Huddlestone, Eugene L. "The Spanish Gipsy and La Gitanilla: An Unnoticed Borrowing." NQ 210 (1965): 103-4. Discusses the play's possible debts to Cervantes' La Gitanilla and to La Fuerza de la Sangre.

327 Hunter, G.K. "The Marking of Sententiae in Elizabethan Printed Plays, Poems, and Romances." Library (series 5) 6 (1951): 171-88. Notes "gnomic pointing" marking moral precepts in a number of Middleton's plays published in the early seventeenth century; suggests that while systematic pointing indicates editorial intent, sporadic pointing may be that of a compositor. Also notes the pointing in the Crane manuscript of A Game at Chess.

328 Jackson, MacD[onald] P. "Affirmative Particles in Henry VIII." Discusses the value of "ay," "yea," and "yes" as differentiators of authorship; argues from an analysis of Middleton's and Tourneur's usage for Middleton's authorship of The Revenger's Tragedy.

329 ----------. "An Allusion to Marlowe's The Jew of Malta in an Early Seventeenth-Century Pamphlet Possibly by Thomas Middleton." NQ 226 (1982): 132-3. Discusses Platoes Cap, a "satirical mock-almanac" dated 1604, its possible authorship by Middleton, and an apparent reference to Marlowe's play.

330 ----------. "Compositorial Practices in The Revenger's Tragedy, 1607-08." Discusses the printing of the 1607-08 edition, looking for proof of Middleton's authorship; finds evidence for two compositors and argues that the play exhibits "strong orthographical and linguistic links with Middleton's holograph of A Game at Chess," evidence that the copy for the quarto of Revenger's Tragedy was "in Middleton's hand."

331 ----------. "A Non-Shakespearian Parallel to the Comic Mispronunciation of 'Ergo' in Hand D of Sir Thomas More." NQ 216 (1971): 139. Notes the spelling of "argo" for "ergo" in the 1607 quarto of The Phoenix (IV.iii.16 in Bullen edition).

332 Jacobs, Henry E. "The Constancy of Change: Character and Perspective in The Changeling." Texas Studies in Literature and Language 16 (1975): 651-74. Argues that "change is the basis of reality in the play," one of "the few constants"; notes the effects of perspective (from external, internal and audience viewpoints) on the attitude towards changes. Studies the various "changelings"; concludes that De Flores is "a creator of changelings" and helps the play fuse "death and change."

333 Jacobson, Daniel J. "There It Goes'--or Does It? Thunder in The Revenger's Tragedy and a Catch-Phrase in Shakespeare, Marlowe and Middleton." ELN 13 (1975): 6-10. Argues that there is no thunder at Revenger's Tragedy IV.ii.199; "there it goes" is a catch-phrase, a "metaphorical lightning flash of insight." Notes a parallel usage in The Family of Love, IV.iii.22.

334 Janzen, Henry [D.]. "Two Cruxes in Dyce's Edition of Middleton's Blurt Master Constable." ELN 10 (1972): 100-101. Discusses IV.i (in Bullen, ll. 30-32 and 73-75); amends readings (Bullen has following Dyce's readings) by reference to the 1602 quarto. (See also his essay, with David M. Holmes, on "Editing Jacobean Drama," 319; see also Berger's additions to the "cruxes" mentioned, 180.)

335 Jewkes, W.T. "The Nightmares of Internal Evidence in Jacobean Drama." SCN 24 (1966): 4-8. Looks at some of the difficulties in using internal evidence to establish authorship, with particular reference to The Revenger's Tragedy and Murray's book (077). Finds adequate evidence for Tourneur's authorship; concludes that most studies of Revenger's Tragedy authorship will "produce the evidence necessary to support whichever of the two assumptions the student of the plays began with" and so perhaps it is better to leave it alone (see also Nicoll, 440, for his support for this position).

336 Jenkins, Harold. "Cyril Tourneur." RES (o.s.) 17 (1941): 21-36. Argues against Middleton's authorship of The Revenger's Tragedy on the grounds that his "wicked people revel in their wickedness as enthusiastically as Tourneur's--only nowhere in Middleton is there any suggestion, tacit or overt, that it is wickedness at all."

337 Johnson, Gerald D. "The Printing of A Faire Quarrell, Q2." Studies in Bibliography 29 (1976): 288-92. Discusses the printing of the 1622 quarto, the second edition; argues that "the practices used in the production of reprints by a job printer who was engaged in the concurrent printing of several editions" led to several compositorial errors and that the edition indicates the "unsettled and hectic" conditions of the print shop.

338 ----------. "Trollope's Note on Middleton and Rowley's A Fair Quarrel." NQ 216 (1971): 27. Notes that the Dyce edition in the Folger Shakespeare Library was owned by Trollope and annotated by him, dated 31 March 1878. Trollope's annotation denies that Middleton ever "did such work as that of the scenes in which Agar [sic] is concerned--never wrote such poetry or conceived such characters ... [he] understood only the appetite of his audience for low buffoonery" and so wrote only the part of "the roarers and streetwalkers," not the main plot.

339 Johnson, Jeffrey L. "The Spoils of Love and Vengeance: A Study of the Jacobean Revenge Tragedy Motivated by Lust." Xavier University Studies 7.3 (Fall 1968): 31-43. Examines The Revenger's Tragedy ("a savage satire on human nature") and Women Beware Women, whose "faulty structure and stereotyped presentation of character traits" and "no set of coherent ethical standards" make the play "confused and chaotic"; argues that only Ford can produce a unified revenge play about lust.

340 Johnson, Paula. "Dissimulation Anatomized: The Changeling." PQ 56 (1977): 329-37. Discusses Middleton's concern with "the relation of trust and truth," with some mention of the comedies and an analysis of The Changeling.

341 Jones, Fred[eric] L. "Cyril Tourneur." TLS 18 June 1931: 487. A preview of the verse analysis discussed more fully in 342; notes that his discoveries suggest Middleton rather than Tourneur as author of Revenger's Tragedy.

342 ----------. "An Experiment with Massinger's Verse." PMLA 47 (1932): 727-40. Examines Massinger's use of "of" and "to" at the end of lines; tests different playwrights and plays and incidentally concludes that The Revenger's Tragedy cannot be Tourneur's but might be Middleton's, and that Massinger could not have had much part in The Old Law.

343 Jones, Robert C. "Italian Settings and the 'World' of Elizabethan Tragedy." SEL 10 (1970): 251-68. Discusses the "Italy of the Elizabethan imagination" and the way in which Elizabethan plays used Italy as a convention with a pattern of associations rather than as a full setting with the connotations of the real Italy.

344 Jordan, R. "Myth and Psychology in The Changeling." RenD 3 (1970): 157-65. Discusses the development of the "beauty and beast" or "maiden and wild man" myth in the play; concludes that "instead of the beast being revealed as a prince, the process of the story is to reveal that the princess is in fact a beast."

345 Junega, Renu. "The Widow as Paradox and Paradigm in Middleton's Plays." Journal of General Education 34 (1982): 3-19. Uses an examination of the presentation of widows as an example of how Middleton "escapes, and even challenges" Renaissance ideas about women. Studies the actual position of widows in Elizabethan society, using scandals and stories; relates this to Middleton's widows in A Trick to Catch the Old One, No Wit No Help Like a Woman's, More Dissemblers Besides Women, and Women Beware Women, and concludes that Middleton was concerned with "the social and cultural roots of their behavior," providing both "a commentary and an analysis."

346 Kaplan, Joel H. "The Feast Day of Middleton's Loyola." NQ 216 (1971): 27-8. Discusses the induction of A Game at Chess and the reason for Loyola's feast day being given as February 29.

347 ----------. "Middleton's Tamburlaine." ELN 13 (1976): 258-60. Notes that The Triumphs of Integrity has Tamburlaine as one of several "honourable worthies" and "an inspiring example of upward mobility."

348 Kehler, Dorothea. "Middleton and Rowley's The Changeling, V, iii, 175-77." Explicator 26 (1968): item 41. Suggests that the significance of the token in this line is not a ring (see Helton, 301), but "intercourse in the closet," arguing that "if De Flores did possess Beatrice at the crucial moment of discovery and judgment, we can better understand why so hardened a woman should suddenly feel 'tis shame to live' (V. iii. 179)."

349 ----------. "Rings and Jewels in The Changeling." ELN 5 (1968): 15-17. Discusses the play's "clear moral framework"; notes the relationship between sexual innuendo and jewels and concludes that the emblem of the ring "delineate[s] the moral framework of The Changeling."

350 Keyishian, Harry. "A Checklist of Medieval and Renaissance Plays (Excluding Shakespeare) on Film, Tape, and Recording." Research Opportunities in Renaissance Drama 17 (1974): 45-58. (**Popular School Update)

351 Kistner, A.L. and M.K. "I Honest Whore: A Comedy of Blood." Humanities Association Bulletin 23.4 (1972): 23-27. A discussion of the blood imagery in the play: "the lineage, lust, bloodshed, and anger."

352 ----------. "The Spanish Gipsy." Humanities Association Review (a continuation of Humanities Association Bulletin) 25 (1974): 211-224. A discussion of the play as a study of loss of identity and its relationship with sin and darkness; argues that the play concludes with a restoration of identity and virtue.

353 ----------. "The Themes and Structures of A Fair Quarrel." Tennessee Studies in Literature 23 (1978): 31-46. Considers the play's "conflict between appearance and reality," as shown in the word "fair" and the concept of "honor." Concentrates on the playwrights' attitude towards the duelling code, with reference to Middleton's pamphlet The Peacemaker.

354 ----------. "What is Hengist, King of Kent?" Arbeiten aus Anglistik und Amerikanistik 7.2 (1982): 147-59. (**MHRA Bibliography 1982)

355 ----------. "Will, Fate, and the Social Order in Women Beware Women." Essays in Literature (Western Illinois University) 3 (1976): 17-31. Emphasises Bianca's moral decline as she improves her social position; finds that Middleton makes her morally responsible for her actions. (**Popular School Update)

356 ----------. "The Family of Love and The Phoenix: Early Development of a Theme." Essays in Literature (Western Illinois University) 7 (1980): 179-90. (**Popular School Update)

357 ----------. "Thomas Middleton's Symbolic Action." Ariel 11 (1980): 15-29. (**MLA Bibliography 1980 and Popular School Update)

358 Knight, W. Nicholas. "Sex and Law in Middleton's Michaelmas Term." In "Accompaninge the players," pp. 89-108. An extensive discussion of the legal vocabulary and framework of Michaelmas Term, of the satire on lawyers, and of the legal imagery; argues that Middleton's law language is "sophisticated and integrated with his other themes."

359 Kreutz, Irving. "Three Collector's Items." Education Theatre Journal 14 (1962): 141-47. A discussion of the difficulties in presenting "minor" classics to a non-specialist audience; includes a review of the 1961 London production of The Changeling (pp. 145-47).

360 Krzyzanowski, Juliusz. "Conjectural Remarks on Elizabethan Dramatists." NQ 195 (1950): 400-402. Part of a series of articles that discusses various cruxes in Elizabethan plays; this part looks at Bullen's editions of Blurt, Master Constable and The Witch.

361 Lake, David. "The Date of Middleton's More Dissemblers Besides Women." NQ 221 (1976): 219-21. An extensive discussion of the evidence, both external and internal, for the dating of More Dissemblers; concludes that the play "should be dated not 'c. 1615' but 'probably May-June 1619.'" See also his monograph, 147.

362 ----------. "Middleton's Hand in The Puritan: Evidence of Vocabulary and Spelling." NQ 217 (1972): 456-60. An anaylsis comparing vocabulary, contractions and spelling and arguing that the case for Middleton's authorship is "overwhelmingly strong." Suggests that the title page's "W.S." is the unknown author of the original plot, which Middleton revised into its present form.

363 ----------. "The Revenger's Tragedy: Internal Evidence for Tourneur's Authorship Negated." NQ 216 (1971): 455-6. Argues against Foakes's edition (Revels; see note to Revenger's Tragedy listings in Part Five) use of act headings, spellings and contractions as evidence for Tourneur's authorship.

364 ----------. "The Shares of Middleton and Others in A Yorkshire Tragedy." NQ 218 (1973): 456-58. Gives evidence of Middleton's hand in the play, using contractions as examples; notes that the play is a "damnation tragedy" (quoting A.C. Cawley) like Hengist, King of Kent, Women Beware Women and The Changeling. Suggests Wilkins and Shakespeare for collaborators; argues from this for Middleton's involvement in The Revenger's Tragedy and Timon of Athens. (See his monograph, 147.)

365 Lancashire, Anne. "The Second Maiden's Tragedy: Chapman Reconsidered and Rejected." ELN 14 (1977), 174-82. A consideration of the argument for and against Middleton's authorship of the play; concludes that, like Middleton's The Wisdom of Solomon Paraphrased, Second's Maiden's Tragedy is "a highly Christian, homiletic work, concerned with personal salvation and damnation." (Response to Brodwin; see 196.)

366 ----------. "The Second Maiden's Tragedy: A Jacobean Saint's Life." RES (n.s.) 25 (1974): 267-79. A further development of the analysis of the play's homiletic elements made by this author in 365 and in her edition of the play (in which she supports the case for Middleton's authorship; see 622); notes the source of the main plot in the "saint's life" of Sophronia and the other "specific, didactic, religious sources" used in the play and concludes that the play's "moral didacticism" was aimed at the court of James I.

367 ----------. "The Witch: Stage Flop or Political Mistake." In "Accompaninge the players," pp. 161-81. A persuasive and extensively documented argument that Middleton's Witch was not a stage "failure" but rather a politically inappropriate play that was suppressed because of its too-obvious parallel with the Essex divorce scandal. Dates the play at about 1613; suggests that the use of songs from Witch in Macbeth may have been an attempt to profit from the play's notoriety.

368 Lancaster, Marjorie S. "Middleton's Use of the Upper Stage in Women Beware Women." Tulane Studies in English 22 (1977): 69-85. Finds a "sardonic humor that stresses the irony" in the play, rather than the tragedy; discusses Middleton's use of the upper stage to "reflect his character's inverted morality" at various points in the play. Praises Middleton's "mastery of emblematic staging" that juxtaposes "visual and verbal elements" to emphasise the characters' hypocrisy.

369 Larsen, T. "Swinburne on Middleton." TLS 17 June 1939: 357. Gives the notes on Swinburne's copy (in the Vancouver, B.C., Public Library) of Bullen's edition of Middleton's works, covering most of Middleton's plays. (For further discussion of these notes, see Page, 452, and Muir, 431.)

370 Lawrence, Robert G. "A Bibiliographical Study of Middleton and Rowley's The Changeling." Library (series 5) 16 (1961): 37-43. A discussion and bibliographical description of the seventeenth-century edition of the play--the 1653 quarto--and of the variants in title page and publisher between issues, with suggestions about the reasons for these variants. Concludes that in Moseley and Newcomb the play found "a publisher and printer of good repute," who provided an accurate edition.

371 Lawrence, W.J. "Early Substantive Theatre Masques." TLS 8 Dec. 1921: 814. A discussion of the use of masques in plays; suggests that elaborate, extensive masques were reserved for court performances only, as the regular stages had no special facilities. Describes the first "independent masque"--Middleton and Rowley's The World Tost at Tennis--and argues that, while written as a "Court Masque," it was never performed at court and that its stage directions suggest its public performance, perhaps in an inn.

372 ----------. "The Mystery of Macbeth: A Solution." In his Shakespeare's Workshop. New York: Haskell House, 1966. Pp. 24-38. Discusses the relationship of Jonson's Masque of Queens (which contained an "Antimasque of Witches") of 1609, Middleton's The Witch (dated at 1608), and the revisions of Macbeth, with special reference to the Hecate scenes. (A reprint of an article that originally appeared in the Fortnightly Review; see Lancashire, 367, for a recent alternative.)

373 ----------. "Notes on a Collection of Masque Music." *Music and Letters* 3 (1922): 49-58. Discusses British Museum additional manuscript 10444, a collection of masque and dance tunes; lists the contents, with comments, and gives the music for "The Second Witches' Dance," which he identifies with Middleton's *The Witch* and *Macbeth*. (For a revised list and comments, see Cutts, 231.)

374 Lehr, John. "Two Names in Middleton's *Michaelmas Term*." *ELN* 18 (1980/81): 15-19. A discussion of the meaning of Hellgill ("the chasm through which an infernal river [Lethe, in this play] flows") and Ephestian ("citizen" or one who is "at home"), with a comment on the overall "social breakdown" of the play's society. (See Levin, 391, for further comments on Quomodo's name.)

375 Lerner, Laurence. "Literature and Money." *E&S* 28 (1975): 106-22. Discusses the two Renaissance viewpoints on money, the moral and the functional; a useful and detailed summary.

376 Levin, Richard. "'The Ass in Compound': a Lost Pun in Middleton, Ford, and Jonson." *ELN* 4 (1967): 12-15. Discusses the pun on "alas," "all ass," "a lass" and names ending in -as (eg. Judas) in various plays.

377 ----------. "The Dampit Scenes in *A Trick to Catch the Old One*." *MLQ* 25 (1964), 140-52. A study of the "coherent sequence of scenes" that show an "Hogarthian 'Usurer's Progress'"; argues that, although the morality and comedy are "imperfectly assimilated," Dampit draws off "the audience's normal detestation of the usurer" from the play's other, more comic, usurers, Lucre and Hoard. (Part of Levin's series of articles, a listing of which follows, on Middleton's multiple plots; most of the material discussed in these articles is contained in his book on the *Multiple Plot* (070).)

378 ----------. "Dekker's Back-Door'd Italian and Middleton's Hebrew Pen." *NQ* 208 (1963): 338-40. Gives further examples to support Turner's sexual interpretation of "back door'd Italian" (see 547) and notes relationship with *Game at Chess*'s "hebrew pen" (see further his monograph, 070).

379 ----------. "The Double Plot of *The Second Maiden's Tragedy*." *SEL* 3 (1963): 219-31. Describes the contrasting, but similarly structured, triangular plots of the play; notes that the women have opposite moral characters and so, as in *The Changeling*, the subplot places the main plot in perspective.

380 ----------. "Elizabethan 'Clown' Subplots." EIC 16 (1966): 84-91. Surveys the different ways in which clown "episodes" are used in Elizabethan plays; discusses, among others, Middleton's The Old Law (clown plot makes main plot actions "more culpable"), A Chaste Maid in Cheapside (the clown lovers are foils for the main lovers), A Fair Quarrel (the Roaring School emphasises the Colonel's exaggerated code of honour) and The Family of Love.

381 ----------. "The Elizabethan 'Three-Level' Play." RenD (n.s.) 2 (1969): 23-37. Discusses those plays which add to the main and subplot a "clown plot"; notes a hierarchy of moods, from romance to realism and satire to farce, in the change between the three plots. Refers to The Family of Love, The Old Law, and A Fair Quarrel for examples.

382 ----------. "The Family of Lust and The Family of Love." SEL 6 (1966): 309-322. Notes the double plot structure of the play, with a "clown" plot extra, an "anti-masque, as in Chaste Maid. Discusses the parallel nature of the play's scenes and the type and theme of each plot .

383 ----------. "The Four Plots of A Chaste Maid in Cheapside." RES (n.s.) 16 (1965): 14-24. Describes the four plots of the play; identifies the parallels between them and the type of plot each represents. Finds that the juxtaposition emphasises the "comic miracle expressed in the title."

384 ----------. "The Lady and her Horsekeeper: Middleton or Rowley?" NQ 208 (1963): 303-6. Discusses the "lady and her stable groom" image of Wit at Several Weapons and its folklore background; considers the possible authorship of the plot.

385 ----------. "'Littera Canina' in Romeo and Juliet and Michaelmas Term." NQ 207 (1962): 333-4. Discusses the pun implicit in the written "R's", as used possibly in Romeo and Juliet and obviously in Michaelmas Term.

386 ----------. "Middleton's Way with Names in A Chaste Maid in Cheapside." NQ 210 (1965): 102-103. Notes the various puns and allusions in the names given the characters of Chaste Maid (a response to Power, 465).

387 ----------. "Mistress Quickly's Case." NQ 211 (1966): 293. Gives examples, including Middleton's plays, of the bawdy use of "my case."

388 ----------. "Name Puns in The Family of Love." NQ 210 (1965): 340-42. Notes at all characters in the play have comic names except Maria and Gerardine, and that each character's name is in some way a pun on his profession or personality.

389 ----------. "'Nuns' and 'Nunnery' in Elizabethan Drama." NQ 213 (1968): 248-49. Notes the use of the sexual double meaning of "nunnery" in Middleton's The Black Book.

390 ----------. "Proverbial Phrases in the Titles of Middleton's Plays." San Francisco Quarterly 28 (1964): 142-45. Notes the prevalence of phrases such as "anything for a quiet life" in the titles of Middleton's plays.

391 ----------. "Quomodo's Name in Michaelmas Term." NQ 218 (1973): 460-61. Notes that "quomodo" means "how"; suggests that the original of Quomodo was a W. Howe convicted by the Star Chamber of a swindle in 1596. Also notes that the word "how" is juxtaposed with Quomodo's name in I.i. and V.iii. (For a comment on Quomodo's first name, see Lehr, 374.)

392 ----------. "The Three Quarrels of A Fair Quarrel." SP 61 (1964): 219-31. Notes that the play contains three quarrels, each involving an insulter, a woman and a defender, although "each plot focuses upon a different aspect of the situation"; suggests that each plot acts and comments on the other two.

393 ----------. "The Unity of Elizabethan Multiple-Plot Drama." English Literary History 34 (1967): 425-46. An overview of "the different senses in which two or more lines of action" are "'related' or 'unified'"; gives his classification system (see his book, 070) of "coordinative," "causal," "analogical," and "affective" links.

394 Levine, Robert T. "Rare Use of 'Since' in Middleton's The Widow and A Chaste Maid in Cheapside." NQ 216 (1971): 457-8. Notes a variation in the punctuation of Widow I.i.84-7 between Bullen's edition and the 1652 quarto; suggests an adverbial usage for "since" which is apparent in another place in Widow and once in Chaste Maid.

395 Lieblein, Leonore. "Thomas Middleton's Prodigal Play." CompD 10 (1976): 54-60. Discusses the development of the Elizabethan prodigal play, with an emphasis on Middleton's A Mad World, My Masters; notes that in the play, both youth and age are in need of "admonition," inverting the relationships in more traditional plays while maintaining the conservative ending.

396 Linthicum, M. Channing. "Gingerline." *PQ* 9 (1930): 212-13. Suggests that the colour of "gingerline," used in *Anything for a Quiet Life* II.ii.5, may be not ginger, but more reddish; examines the derivation of the word.

397 Lisca, Peter. "*The Revenger's Tragedy*: A Study in Irony." *PQ* 38 (1959): 242-51. An extensive discussion of the irony in the play; treats the play as by Tourneur, but notes that the quantity and use of irony possibly "strengthens the argument" for Middleton's authorship. (The essay is reprinted in *Shakespeare's Contemporaries*, pp. 307-17.)

398 Lloyd, Bertram. "A Minor Source of *The Changeling*." *MLR* 19 (1924): 101-2. Notes that as well as Reynolds's *God's Revenge*, Middleton may have used Lenerd Digges's novel (translated from the Spanish of Cespedes) *Gerardo the Unfortunate Spaniard* (London, 1922).

399 Lockert, Lucy. "The Greatest of Elizabethan Melodramas." In *Essays in Dramatic Literature*: The Parrott Presentation Volume, ed. Hardin Craig. Princeton: Princeton University Press, 1935. Pp. 103-26. Argues that *The Revenger's Tragedy* is "the supreme melodrama in all the literature of the world"; discusses authorship briefly in a note, leaning towards Middleton.

400 Marotti, Arthur F. "Fertility and Comic Form in *A Chaste Maid in Cheapside*." *Comparative Drama* 3 (1969), 65-74. Argues that the play shows "a spirit of vitality and play that distracts the audience from the potential moral issues in such rambunctious sexuality"; sees Sir Walter as a "scapegoat figure," carrying off the "moral disgust the audience might feel for any of the play's other vicious characters."

401 ----------."The Method in the Madness of *A Mad World, My Masters*." *Tennessee Studies in Literature* 15 (1970), 99-108. Argues that the play's "recreative mirth" is generated by "the monomania of the characters and the playworld's comic disorder"; feels that Penitent is as "ludicrously self-righteous" in his repentance as he was ridiculous in his "previous cliche libertinism." (For another view on Penitent's seriousness see Hallett, 295, and Parker, 453, among others.)

402 ----------."The Purgations of Middleton's The Family of Love." PLL 7 (1970): 80-84. Discusses the various forms of purgation in the play; concludes that by the end of the play, society, in which "moral diseases have a kind of physical definition," has been purged and can celebrate the "festive conclusion" of the marriage.

403 Mathews, Ernst G. "The Murdered Substitute Tale." MLQ 6 (1945): 187-95. Discusses the origins of the plot involving Diaphanta in The Changeling.

404 Maxwell, Baldwin. "The Date of Middleton's Women Beware Women." PQ 22 (1943), 338-42. Dates the play at c. 1621 because of allusions to events of 1621. (See Cope, 222, for refutation of this.)

405 ----------."Middleton's Michaelmas Term." PQ 22 (1943): 29-35. Discusses the contemporary references in the play; dates the play therefore at 1605-6. Notes that as Paul's Boys disappear in July 1606, "Middleton's play may have contributed to the boys' downfall."

406 ----------. "Middleton's The Phoenix." John Quincy Adams Memorial Studies, pp. 743-53. Dates Phoenix as 1603, probably summer, or June to December generally, using contemporary references within the play as evidence. Sees the play as a transition between Blurt, Master Constable and the satiric plays about London life.

407 ----------. "A Note on the Date of Middleton's The Family of Love, with a Query on the Porters Hall Theatre." In Elizabethan Studies and Other Essays in Honor of George F. Reynolds. Boulder, Colo.: University of Colorado Studies, 1945 (Studies in the Humanities, Vol. 2, No. 4). Pp. 195-200. Argues with Bald's date for Family (see 167). Describes a reference to "the whole new livery of porters" in Family I.iii and IV.iii; notes that the Company of Porters was apparently reorganised in Spring 1605 and given a hall and so therefore the play should be dated later than June 1605, after the publication of a ballad praising the porters.

408 ----------. "The Old Law." In his Studies in Beaumont, Fletcher, and Massinger. Chapel Hill: University of North Carolina Press, 1939. Pp. 138-146. Discusses the stage history and dating of the play; rejects Morris's suggestions about composition (see 428) and suggests a date of 1618 for the writing of the play, with Middleton and Rowley the authors, and a possible slight influence from Massinger, perhaps as the reviser when the play was presented at court in 1625.

409 ----------. "Thomas Middleton's _Your Five Gallants_." _PQ_ 30 (1951): 30-39. A general discussion of the play, with emendations suggested in the ordering of scenes (IV.i and IV.ii should precede III) in Dyce and Bullen and the suggestion of a date (1606 or 1607 at earliest). Comments that Middleton is a satirist rather than a dramatist in this play: he provides "no well-drawn comic figure" and ignores unifying devices because he is "so intent upon his castigation of contemporary abuses."

410 ----------. "'Twenty Good-Nights'--_The Knight of the Burning Pestle_ and Middleton's _Family of Love_." _MLN_ 63 (1948): 233-37. Finds a parody of _Family of Love_ in _Knight_--the device of the lover in the coffin. Accepts the Maria-Gerardine plot as intentionally romantic, not satiric, and concludes therefore that Beaumont is "ridiculing not only the devices of romantic drama but the language in which Middleton had written." (See reponse by Olive, 449, and Olive's original suggestion, 450.)

411 Maxwell, J.C. "Desperate Debts." _NQ_ 212 (1967): 141. Discusses the two kinds of debts, "sperate" debts, which had hopes of being repaid, and "desperate," or irrecoverable, ones. Notes the uses of the term "desperate" in _Michaelmas Term_.

412 ----------. [Untitled letter.] _NQ_ 218 (1973): 470. Notes an authority for his suggested emendation in _Women Beware Women_ II.ii.181 (see his review of Gomme, 583, for his first suggestion of this).

413 McBride, Margaret M. "Berryman's 'World's Fair.'" _Explicator_ 34 (1975): item 22. Notes allusions to _A Chaste Maid in Cheapside_ in Berryman's poem, and the poet's use of the play in his parent-child and swan imagery.

414 McCanles, Michael. "The Moral Dialectic of Middleton's _Women Beware Women_." In "_Accompaninge the players_," pp. 203-218. Discusses the "links between cause and effect" in the play, arguing that "the causal relation between human moral qualities and motivations [is] defined as mutually exclusive of each other." Includes diagrammes to show that "immorality in this play is ... both interdicted by moral imperatives and caused by them," as "human good and evil both exclude and imply each other."

415 McCarten, John. "Kindergarten in the Village." New Yorker 7 Nov. 1964: 99. A review of Kazan's production of The Changeling, about "a young Spanish girl [who] doesn't want to marry the fellow her dad has chosen for her." See Brustein's comments on this production, and on his fellow critics who did not understand the play (202).

416 McCullen, Joseph T., Jr. "The Use of Parlor and Tavern Games in Elizabethan and Early Stuart Drama. MLQ 14 (1953): 7-14. Discusses the role of games, especially dice and chess, in "promoting dramatic action" and variety.

417 McElroy, John F. "Middleton, Entertainer or Moralist? An Interpretation of The Family of Love and Your Five Gallants." MLQ 37 (1976): 35-46. Insists that Middleton wrote for "entertainment, not instruction"; uses his early plays as proof, assuming that they "reveal his intentions more nakedly than the later and better works." Argues that Family of Love is a parody of romantic comedy, Phoenix a satire, with no ethical basis, and Gallants a farce. Concludes that these plays offer "little for the intellect to ponder and still less for the conscience to feed upon." (See further his monograph, 148.)

418 McManaway, J[ames] G. "Fortune's Wheel." TLS 16 April 1938: 264. Notes Middleton's confusion of Fortune's wheel with the wheel of the Fates in Lucrece (l. 402; also noted in the Adams edition) and in Roaring Girl (Q 1611 sig B4).

419 ----------. "Latin Title-Page Mottoes as a Clue to Dramatic Authorship." Library (series 4) 26 (1945): 28-36. Notes the existence of a copy of the Blurt, Master Constable quarto with scribal additions to replace missing leaves; uses the information in conjunction with title-page Latin mottoes to identify the company producing the anonymous Dick of Devonshire and to suggest an author.

420 ----------. "Thomas Dekker: Further Textual Notes." Library (series 4) 19 (1938): 176-79. Further discussion of the Dyce copy of Roaring Girl (see Bowers, 188); argues that Bowers's argument puts "running-titles" ahead of textual evidence. (See Bowers, 189, for the final word on this discussion; he reverses his stand.)

421 Mehl, Dieter. "Emblems in English Renaissance Drama." RenD (n.s.) 2 (1969): 39-57. Defines emblems and studies the interrelation between drama and emblem; discusses The Changeling, Women Beware Women, The Revenger's Tragedy and the pageants.

422 Messina, Joseph. "The Moral Design of A Trick to Catch the Old One." In "Accompaninge the players," pp. 109-32. Discusses Middleton's integration, in this play, of moral theme and festive mood; argues that "it is the Dampit scenes that give the play its ethical basis," because Dampit, a "grotesque," offers "a reality of evil and grotesquerie" in which a sinner can suffer and be damned, and thus balances the "tolerant ethical attitude" in the festive main plot.

423 Mincoff, Marco K. The Authorship of The Revenger's Tragedy." Studia Historico-Philologica-Serdicensia 2 (1939): 1-87. A study of the imagery of The Revenger's Tragedy that suggests Middleton as author in place of Tourneur; a frequently discussed article in a reasonably obscure journal. (See Ellis-Fermor, 261, for a similar study with opposite results.) (**Popular School and many other citations)

424 Mooney, Michael E. "'The Common Sight' and Dramatic Form: Rowley's Embedded Jig in A Faire Quarrel." SEL 20 (1980): 305-323. Discusses the use of "brief farces that were integrated into the structure of plays"; argues that IV.iv of Fair Quarrel is one such that "complete[s] the pattern of multiple reflecting plots" by emphasising "the travesty of the heroic ethic so celebrated in the main plot."

425 ----------. "'Framing' as Collaborative Technique: Two Middleton-Rowley Plays." Comparative Drama 13 (1979): 127-141. Argues that, in A Fair Quarrel and The Changeling, Middleton and Rowley used "framing" to organise their collaboration; Rowley wrote the beginning and ending and the subplot and Middleton the main plot. Notes the balance between the two contributors, and the ways in which each plot considers parallel events and language; suggests that Rowley "constructed the plays" while Middleton "tapped the potential psychological tensions."

426 Moore, John Robert. "The Contemporary Significance of Middleton's Game at Chesse." PMLA 50 (1935): 761-8. Describes the title page of the first two quartos; discusses the associations of chess and the political references of the play. Suggests Buckingham as the play's sponsor. (For a rejection of this, see Heinemann, 300.)

427 Morris, Edgar Coit. "The Allegory in Middleton's A Game at Chesse." Englishe Studien 38 (1907): 39-52. A comprehensive discussion of the allegory in the play, with all characters identified.

428 ----------. "On the Date and Composition of The Old Law." PMLA 17 (1902): 1-70. Discusses Middleton, Rowley, and Massinger's personal styles and on that basis assigns the play line by line; concludes that the only composition manner that fits his division would be an original play by Middleton (written about 1599), revised by Rowley about 1616, and then revised again by Massinger about 1625.

429 Morrison, Peter. "A Cangoun in Zombieland: Middleton's Teratological Changeling." In "Accompaninge the players," pp. 219-241. Includes a bibliography on The Changeling. Argues that the play is of "indeterminant genre" yet is "a great play that openly flaunts its flaws." Finds the heart of the play to be, not change, but madness; suggests that it is a "monster story: the monster loses, but the winners are frauds"--zombies. Derives "changeling" from "cangoun," the deformed, exchanged child, and identifies De Flores as the only changeling in the play, the "terribly beautiful and horrible" true self of mankind. Concludes that the play demands "personal action and commitment to the reformation of man" but "leaves little doubt as to what its author thinks the real chances are." A highly provocative essay.

430 Muir, Kenneth. "The Role of Livia in Women Beware Women." In Poetry and Drama 1570-1700: Essays in Honour of Harold F. Brooks, ed. Antony Coleman and Antony Hammond. London: Methuen, 1981. Pp. 76-89. Argues that Women Beware Women is "surely" a "better play" than The Changeling; discusses Livia, who "unites the two main plots," and manipulates and destroys the "initially innocent" Bianca and Isabella.

431 ----------. "Swinburne on Middleton." TLS 24 Feb. 1945: 91. Comments on the notes detailed by Larsen (see 399); observes that the wording is identical with the wording in Swinburne's article and questions their authorship. Also makes two emendations of Bullen's text, in Phoenix I.ii.78-84 and Michaelmas Term IV.i.63.

432 ----------. "Two Plays Reconsidered: More Dissemblers Besides Women and No Wit, No Help Like a Woman's." In "Accompaninge the players," pp. 147-59. Discusses the two plays, "which are, in their different ways, masterly," although not without weaknesses, and which deserve more attention. Argues that they are theatrical plays, not poetical ones, and hence the reason for their unjustified neglect.

433 Mulholland, P.A. "The Date of The Roaring Girl." RES (n.s.) 28 (1977): 18-31. Argues that past dates (1604-5,1607-8) have been based on an incorrectly dated trial record; suggests that the correct date, January 1611/12, and references in the trial transcript suggest late April or early May, 1611, for the date of performance.

434 ----------. "Notes on Several Derivations of Crane's Manuscript of Middleton's The Witch." PBSA 78 (1984): 75-81. Discusses various appearances of editions or parts of The Witch that derive from Crane's manuscript; notes that Reed's edition of the play (1778, the first printing) was set from George Steeven's transcription (now in the Folger Library). Also notes Witch extracts in Reed's edition of Shakespeare (1778) and in the 1673-1674 editions of Shakespeare (because of the link with Macbeth).

435 ----------. "Some Textual Notes on The Roaring Girl." Library (series 5) 32 (1977): 333-43. Discusses the 1611 quarto; revises some readings and adds more variants; conjectures that the printer's copy was non-theatrical in origin--perhaps a fair copy by either or both dramatists, made especially for the printer. Also mentions a new copy of the play in Corpus Christi College, Oxford.

436 Mulryne, J.R. "Annotations in Some Copies of Two New Playes by Thomas Middleton, 1657." Library (series 5) 30 (1975): 217-21. Discusses some annotated copies of this first printing of both plays, including what appear to be notes on a performance.

437 ----------. "The French Source for the Sub-plot of Middleton's Women Beware Women." RES (n.s.) 25 (1974): 439-45. Discusses the two French versions and the English version of the story of Hippolito and Isabella; suggests that, although he cannot be certain, Middleton was "probably indebted" to the French text now in the Arsenal Library in Paris.

438 ----------. "Half-Sheet Imposition and Running-Title Transfer in Two New Playes by Thomas Middleton, 1657." Library (series 5) 30 (1975): 222-28. Reviews the evidence for half-sheet imposition in gatherings A and O of this edition, with reference to running titles; discusses the printing methods. (A further discussion of "The Impositon of Initial and Final Half-Sheets in an Octavo" is contained in the article that follows this one--Library 30, pp. 229-32.)

439 ----------. "Manuscript Source-Material for the Main Plot of Thomas Middleton's Women Beware Women." YES 5 (1975): 70-74. Discusses fourteen possible Italian manuscript sources for the Bianca Cappello story used in the play.

440 Nicoll, Allardyce. "The Revenger's Tragedy and the Virtue of Anonymity." Essays on Shakespeare and the Elizabethan Drama in Honor of Hardin Craig, ed. Richard Holsley. Columbia: University of Missouri Press, 1962. Pp. 309-16. Summarises the debate to 1962; presents a most persuasive case for leaving the play anonymous: "May not emphasis upon authorship tend to close our eyes to other and more significant considerations?"

441 Nosworthy, J.M. "Macbeth at the Globe." Library (series 5) 2 (1947): 108-118. Discusses Macbeth in performance compared with the text in the First Folio; suggests that the text has perhaps some minor cuts but "Macbeth never [was] anything but a short play." Incidentally denies Middleton any responsibility for the Hecate scenes.

442 Oliphant, E.H.C. "Anything for a Quiet Life." NQ 142 (1922): 11. Supports Sykes's attributions, with slightly different scene divisions. (See Sykes's extensive discussion of the play, 538.)

443 ----------. "The Authorship of The Revenger's Tragedy." SP 23 (1926): 157-68. The first major attribution of the play to Middleton, based on style, versification, parallels with other Middleton plays, and other textual evidence. Also gives Blurt Master Constable to Dekker. (See Foakes--274--for refutation of the versification evidence.)

444 ----------. "The Bloodie Banquet: A Dekker-Middleton Play." TLS 17 Dec. 1925: 882. Discusses evidence for Dekker's authorship (play attribution "T.D.") and Middleton's collaboration; assigns scenes. Finds the play a "horrible and disjointed, but powerful and interesting tragedy."

445 ----------. "Problems of Authorship in Elizabethan Dramatic Literature." MP 8 (1911): 411-459. A survey of the various kinds of anonymous, semi-anonymous, or controversial plays of the period; lists the plays worth a study of authorship, including The Revenger's Tragedy, and mentions Middleton as a possible candidate for its author.

446 ----------. "Tourneur and Mr. Eliot." SP 32 (1935): 546-52. Surveys the support for Middleton's authorship of The Revenger's Tragedy and attacks Eliot's arguments; insists on the difference between Atheist's Tragedy and Revenger's Tragedy. (A response to Eliot's article on Tourneur in TLS 1930, and to Eliot's response to Oliphant in TLS 1931; see 260.)

447 ----------. "Tourneur and The Revenger's Tragedy." TLS 18 December 1930: 1037. A reassessment (a response to Eliot's review; see 260) of his evidence for Middleton's authorship; moderates his views somewhat (he agrees that Middleton "never shows any concern whatever with moral problems" while the author of the Revenger's Tragedy is "markedly a moralist"), but still prefers Middleton on the ground of stylistic evidence.

448 ----------. "Tourneur and The Revenger's Tragedy." TLS 5 Feb. 1931: 99. A response to the anonymous (actually by Eliot) Jan. 1, 1931 article; discusses the accuracy of the order of Stationer's Register entries as guides to the dating of plays.

449 Olive, W.J. "'Twenty Good Nights'--The Knight of the Burning Pestle, The Family of Love, and Romeo and Juliet." SP 47 (1950): 182-89. Notes parodies of Shakespeare in Knight and possibly in Family of Love; points out that Family of Love is itself a burlesque--or at least an imitation--of Romeo and Juliet. (A response to Maxwell, 408.)

450 ----------. "Imitation of Shakespeare in Middleton's The Family of Love." PQ 29 (1950): 75-8. Notes the various elements of Middleton's play that are borrowed from Romeo and Juliet and 1 Henry IV; comments on other verbal echoes of Shakespeare in Middleton's work.

451 Ornstein, Robert. "The Ethical Design of The Revenger's Tragedy." English Literary History 21 (1954), 81-93. A general discussion of the play, accepting Tourneur as author. Finds in the play "a world of rogues and scoundrels in which moral law seems absent or ineffectual" yet which is governed by "a moral order, detached and ironic, which operates through ... human psychology."

452 Page, Frederick. "Swinburne on Middleton." TLS 8 July, 1939: 406. Comments that the notes detailed in Larsen's article (399) were included in Swinburne's article on Middleton in Nineteenth Century for January 1886 (reprinted in his Age of Shakespeare, 1908, and as the introduction to the Mermaid edition, ed. Ellis, 1887--see 580.

453 Parker, R.B. "Middleton's Experiments with Comedy and Judgement." Jacobean Theatre, ed. J.R. Brown and Bernard Harris. London: Edward Arnold, 1960. Pp. 178-99. An extensive study of the comedies, illustrating Parker's thesis that Middleton's style contains "a tension between skill in the presentation of manners and a desire to denounce immorality." Relates this to the tragedies as well and concludes that "Middleton's comic world thus has two polarities: a completely amoral vitalism and a more than Calvinistically determined scheme of retribution." An important study, frequently cited by other critics.

454 Paster, Gail Kern. "The City in Plautus and Middleton." RenD (n.s.) 6 (1973): 29-44. Discusses the similarities in perspective and atmosphere between Plautus' comedies and Middleton's; notes that both rely on the "sense of actuality of a specifically urban background." Examines Middleton's main comedies extensively; concludes that "the cruel mechanization of personal relationships is intimately tied to the greater urban world."

455 Pentzell, Raymond J. "The Changeling: Notes on Mannerism in Dramatic Form." Comparative Drama 9 (1975): 3-28. Notes the awkwardness of the final scene and questions the subplot; discusses the varieties in tone and the juxtaposition of different "stage realities." Suggests "mannerism" as a useful term and defines it as an "extreme tension between totally manipulative artifice ... and 'the shock of recognition.'"

456 Peter, John. "The Revenger's Tragedy Reconsidered." EIC 6 (1956), 131-143. Considers Tourneur as a moralist; Comments that "whatever his claims to our sympathy or interest" Vindice's "moral commentary on the villanies around him" sets up a standard "by which he himself is condemned." (See response by Craik--228.)

457 ----------. Response to Craik's "The Revenger's Tragedy" (EIC 6:482-5--see 228). EIC 6 (1956): 485-6. Peter answers that "all I wished to suggest was that Tourneur would not have punished the brothers if they'd seemed to him innocent."

458 Phelps, Wayne H. "Thomas Holmes, Esquire: The Dedication of Middleton's The Witch." NQ 225 (1980): 152-54. Discusses the dedication on the manuscript presentation copy (the Ralph Crane transcript) and reviews the candidates for "Thomas Holmes."

459 Phialas, P.G. "Middleton's Early Contact with the Law." SP 52 (1955), 186-194. Discusses a suit by Middleton's step-father Thomas Harvey against Middleton's mother; notes that Middleton was in London early in 1600.

460 ----------. "Middleton and Munday." TLS 23 Nov. 1956: 697. Notes the pageant rivalry between Middleton and Munday from 1605 to 1626; mentions shared pageant in 1623 and gives an example of their competition in 1619 (see also, Withington, 128 and 571, Bergeron, 009, and Welsford, 124).

461 ----------. "An Unpublished Letter about A Game at Chesse." MLN 69 (1954): 398-9. Gives the text of a letter, written in August 1624, from Don Carlos Colona (the Spanish Ambassador) to King James, complaining about "une comedie si scandaleuse, impie, barbare, et si offensive." (For more from Don Carlos, see Wilson and Turner, 569.)

462 Pineas, Rainer. "A Missing Source-Book for Middleton's A Game at Chesse." NQ 210 (1965): 353-4. A discussion of V.iii.147-8; notes that the story was general in "contemporary Protestant polemics", available in many sources and therefore no one source-book. (A response to Southall, 527; see also Yachnin, 575.)

463 Potter, John. "'In Time of Sports': Masques and Masking in Middleton's Women Beware Women." PLL 18 (1982): 368-383. Finds in the play a "series of social ceremonies" that "give significance to the action," reflecting Middleton's experience as writer of public festivals; discusses the pattern of Bianca's "loss of innocence" and argues that the final masque is "an integral part of the play."

464 Power, William. "Double, double." NQ 204 (1959): 4-8. A survey of the possible authorship clues in duplicated first names in The Roaring Girl and Anything for a Quiet Life. Commments about Quiet Life that "one of Middleton's distinguishing characteristics is his intellectual honesty. Anything for a Quiet Life is not honest"; feels that the evidence for a collaborator is strong.

465 ----------. "Middleton's Way with Names." NQ 205 (1960): 26-9, 56-60, 95-8, 136-40 and 175-79. A discussion of the meanings and allusions of the names of some of Middleton's characters, including a discussion of repeated names and of odd or unusual names, of the names in The Changeling, and of Middleton's family names, with some speculation about his wife's (or wives') name. (See also Levin's articles, expecially 386, for naming allusions.)

466 ----------. "The Phoenix, Raleigh, and King James." NQ 203 (1958): 57-61. An investigation of the political aspects of the play: finds it "a determined attack upon Sir Walter Ralegh [sic], and an attempt to make a romantic hero out of King James himself." Finds also a discussion of the duties and responsibilities of kings that agrees essentially with James's Basilikon Doron, and concludes that "the reign was only a few months old, and it was still possible to hope for great things from the new monarch." (The second part of an extended discussion about Phoenix; see further Bawcutt (178) and Dodson (238).)

467 ----------. "Thomas Middleton vs. King James I." NQ 202 (1957): 526-34. Traces the changing attitudes towards the King shown in Middleton's plays, from The Phoenix's praise of him (see 2.145) through the Scottish satire of Michaelmas Term to the "final episode" of A Game at Chess: "In 1603 Englishmen hoped that James would improve upon Elizabeth; in 1624 they hoped that Charles would improve upon James."

468 Price, George R. "The Authorship and the Bibliography of The Revenger's Tragedy." Library (series 5) 15 (1960): 262-277. An analysis of the textual evidence for the authorship of the play and "a full bibliographical analysis" of the 1607 quarto. Argues for Middleton's authorship, focussing especially on a comparison of the punctuation with the punctuation, on the one hand, of first editions of Middleton's plays and, on the other, of works known to be by Tourneur.

469 ----------. "The Authorship and the Manuscript of The Old Law." Huntingdon Library Quarterly 16 (1953): 117-39. Divides the play between Middleton and Rowley, but feels that it was much revised by Massinger; dates the play at 1614 or 1615.

470 ----------. "Compositors' Methods With Two Quartos Reprinted by Augustine Mathewes." PBSA 44 (1950): 269-74. Discusses the composition of the second quarto of A Fair Quarrel, set from the second issue of Quarto 1; finds evidence for two compositors, one more careful than the other.

471 ----------. "Dividing the Copy for Michaelmas Term." PBSA 60 (1966): 327-36. Notes that two printers published the play; discusses the setting and printing of the play and the method of casting off and dividing the copy. Comments that the pages were set consecutively by printer A and by formes by printer B; suggests that the printers' copy was Middleton's fair copy or a very faithful scribal transcript.

472 ----------. "The Early Editions of A Trick to Catch the Old One." Library (series 5) 22 (1967): 205-27. An "account of the major facts about the composition and printing of the play" which also examines evidence in the text "which indicates the nature of the printer's copy"; he concludes that the first edition was probably Middleton's "fair copy," taken from Blackfriars' "theatre files," and notes its two issues, the second with a cancel title-page. Notes the mistakes and garbled wording in the second edition and finds its form hard to describe; suggests that it was based on the first edition.

473 ----------. "Early Editions of The Ant and the Nightingale." PBSA 43 (1949): 179-90. Suggests that STC 17881 is the first edition and 17880 the second edition; notes that 17881 is shortened (no "Scholar's Tale"). Discusses the variants between the editions and the printing methods; describes a possible scenario explaining why the work had two different publishers but the same printer. (See Shaaber--518--for a discussion of the same evidence, with different conclusions.)

474 ----------. "The First Edition of A Faire Quarrell." Library (series 5) 4 (1949): 137-41. Discusses the first edition--publisher, stationer, printer--with a full bibliographical description and a discussion of printing methods. Concludes that the copy for issue one was "a fair copy of the authors' manuscript."

475 ----------. "The First Edition of Your Five Gallants and of Michaelmas Term." Library (series 5) 8 (1953): 23-29. A bibliographical description of each play's first edition, with some speculation about the printing of each.

476 ----------. "The Huntingdon MS of *A Game at Chesse*." *Huntingdon Library Quarterly* 17 (1954): 83-8. Notes that Middleton's handwriting may be in evidence on the manuscript.

477 ----------. "The Latin Oration in *A Game at Chesse*." *Huntingdon Library Quarterly* 23 (1960): 398-93. Argues that the oration of the Jesuit in V.i. is based on welcoming oration of a Jesuit to Prince Charles in Madrid in 1623.

478 ----------. "The Manuscript and the Quarto of *The Roaring Girl*." *Library* (series 5) 11 (1956): 180-86. Discusses the 1611 edition and suggests that "the whole play was transcribed especially for the printer" by Dekker. Describes the composition and printing of the play and suggests three to five compositors were involved.

479 ----------. "Medical Men in *A Faire Quarrell*." *Bulletin of the History of Medicine* (Baltimore) 24 (1950): 38-42. (***New Cambridge Bibliography* and *Popular School*)

480 ----------. "The Quartos of *The Spanish Gypsy* [sic] and Their Relation to *The Changeling*." *PBSA* 52 (1958): 111-25. Describes the 1653 and 1661 quartos of *Gipsy* and the "bibliographical clues" connecting them to *The Changeling*; suggests that the copy for Quarto 1 of *Gipsy* was the "theater scribe's fair copy made for submitting to the censor and for annotation by the prompter."

481 ----------. "Setting by Formes in the First Edition of *The Phoenix*." *PBSA* 56 (1962): 414-27. Discusses the evidence in the first quarto of *Phoenix* for setting by formes rather than by consecutive pages; comments also on the reason for press corrections in the outer forme of quire B (Harvard copy). Suggests that the copy was "an early draft" of the play in Middleton's autograph.

482 ----------. "The Shares of Middleton and Dekker in a Collaborated Play." *Papers of the Michigan Academy of Science, Arts, and Letters* 30 (1944): 601-15. A discussion of *The Roaring Girl*. (**Popular School)

483 Price, Hereward T. "The Authorship of *Timon of Athens*." *JEGP* 42 (1943): 55-61. A survey of the tests and choices involved in the various attributions of parts of *Timon*; with Shakespeare and rejects all three. See Lake, 147, and Jackson, 146, for the current arguments that involve Middleton in this discussion.

484 ----------. "Towards a Scientific Method of Textual Criticism for the Elizabethan Drama." JEGP 36 (1937): 151-67. Discusses the various methods of textual criticism--vocabulary, metrical tests, spellings, speech headings, etc.--and ways of improving their reliability.

485 Putt, S. Gorley. "The Tormented World of Middleton." TLS 2 Aug. 1974: 833-4. An extensive review of Farr's monograph (see 141); argues that Beatrice's "sexual recklessness" equals De Flores', and surveys the criticism of the play to show how few critics have appreciated this. Denies any view of Beatrice as initially innocent; she has "a degree of nymphomania" as marked as "De Flores' resemblance to a satyr." Notes that Farr avoids the Revenger's Tragedy authorship controversy.

486 Rabkin, Norman. "The Double Plot: Notes on the History of a Convention." RenD 7 (1964): 55-69. Notes the changes in the convention, from truly unified double-plot plays (including Middleton's) to the double plots of later plays by Beaumont and Fletcher, and of coterie plays by Chapman and by Marston, in which the unity was all but lacking.

487 ----------. "Problems in the Study of Collaboration." Research Opportunities in Renaissance Drama 19 (1976): 7-13. Discusses the problems in dividing The Roaring Girl between Middleton and Dekker and in understanding the successful collaboration of Middleton and Rowley in The Changeling. (**Popular School Update)

488 Reed, Robert R., Jr. "A Factual Interpretation of The Changeling's Madhouse Scenes." NQ 195 (1950): 247-8. Suggests that the asylum scenes are a burlesque of Bethlehem Hospital and of Dr. Hilkish Crooke, who was made steward in 1619. (The suggestion presents a problem in dating: Crooke was not tried for his frauds and abuses until 1632, so it is questionable whether his abuses would be general gossip by 1622 [Bald's date for Changeling, seldom challenged]).

489 Reeves, John D. "Thomas Middleton and Lily's Grammar: Some Parallels." NQ 197 (1952): 75-6. Points out some parallels between the Latin Grammar of William Lily (c. 1540) and quotations in Family of Love and Chaste Maid; suggests that this indicates a grammar school education for Middleton, Lily's being a required text.

490 Ribner, Riving. "Middleton's Women Beware Women: Poetic Imagery and the Moral Vision." Tulane Studies in English 9 (1960): 19-33. Finds the play a "denunciation of a society which has abandoned ethical values and has instead deified worldly success and false appearances," and Middleton's tragic vision "profoundly pessimistic." Argues that his characters are never initially virtuous; they do not really "decline in moral stature ... [but] merely become aware of their own corruption and ... moral equivocation" as they suffer the tragic consequences of their actions.

491 Richards, Bernard. "Corrections and Additions to Recent Editions of Middleton and Rowley's A Fair Quarrel." NQ 225 (1980): 154-55. Adds explanations and additional glosses to the editions by Price and Holdsworth.

492 Richman, David. "Directing Middleton's Comedy." In "Accompaninge the players," pp. 79-88. Discusses a production of A Chaste Maid in Cheapside at the University of Rochester (N.Y.) during the summer of 1978; notes the changes made (the play was set in Regency London) and script alterations made to reinforce Middleton's satire and comedy for a modern audience--the bawdinesss was greatly emphasised.

493 Ricks, Christopher. "The Moral and Poetic Structure of The Changeling." EIC 10 (1960): 290-306. Discusses the double meanings, one sexual, of the words in the play; notes how Beatrice cannot choose one meaning without the other, because each is after all one word, and so links the word-play to the play's theme. (This article and the following listing are frequently referred to by other authors; they are seen as important developments in the understanding of Middleton's dramatic style.)

494 ----------. "Word-Play in Women Beware Women." RES (n.s.) 12 (1961): 239-50. Describes the play as one "about the corruption of life and love by money"; discusses how the worlds of money and love are connected by puns and word games which have "a serious relevance to the moral analysis in the play."

495 Robb, Dewar M. "The Canon of William Rowley's Plays." MLR 45 (1950): 129-41. Points out problems and errors in Rowley scholarship; discusses a possible way in which Middleton and Rowley may have collaborated. Concludes that Rowley's plays with Middleton included The Old Law, A Fair Quarrel, Wit at Several Weapons, The World Tost at Tennis (masque), and The Changeling, and suggests scene divisions for each play.

496 Roberts, Gareth. "A Re-examination of the Sources of the Magical Material in Middleton's The Witch." NQ 221 (1976): 216-19. Surveys various sources already noted for the witch material; gives additional examples of borrowing from Reginald Scot's Discoverie of Witchcraft (1584) and suggests Le Loyer's A Treatise of Specters (trans. 1605) as an additional source.

497 Root, Robert L., Jr. "The Troublesome Reformation of Penitent Brothel: Middletonian Irony and A Mad World, My Masters." College Language Association Journal 25 (1981): 82-90. Sees Penitent as an "introverted conniver" who brings about his own internal reversal, as Follywit the outward conniver causes his own external reversal of fortune. Argues that Penitent as a moral exemplum is flawed; his "pious concerns are an extreme reaction" peculiar to himself. Concludes that the final irony is that order is "re-established through [the deceiver's] own agencies."

498 Rowe, George E., Jr. "The Old Law and Middleton's Comic Vision." English Literary History 42 (1975): 189-202. Notes how Middleton reverses comic expectations and the conventions of "New Comedy" in the play; finds that the "play as a whole passes judgment on the assumptions and logic of comedy itself" and is "the most powerful embodiment of Middleton's comic vision." (See also his monograph, 151.)

499 ----------. "Prodigal Sons, New Comedy, and Middleton's Michaelmas Term." English Literary Renaissance 7 (1977): 90-107. Discusses the play's "unsettling" combination of New Comedy convention and prodigal son pattern; in one, the audience sympathy is with the young, but in the other, with the old. Describes the patterns of the play, and its allegorical framework of city and country; notes the alternating view of Quomodo as "maligned parent" and "crafty draper". Concludes that the play's "disquieting ambiguity" is perhaps the "true hallmark" of Middleton's art. (See also his monograph, 151.)

500 Roy, Emil. "Sexual Paradox in The Changeling." Literature and Psychology 25 (1975): 124-32. A psychoanalytic approach to the play; sees most characters as expressing sexual preoccupations of an Oedipal sort--for example, De Flores "selects a vindictive, hurtful mother figure as love object" when he chooses Beatrice.

501 Sabol, Andrew J. "Ravenscroft's Melismate and the Children of Paul's." Renaissance News 12 (1959): 3-9. Finds the words and music of a song for A Trick to Catch the Old One (sung by Audrey) in this songbook (1611).

502 ----------. "Two Songs with Accompaniment for an Elizabethan Choirboy Play." Studies in the Renaissance 5 (1958): 145-57. Discusses the songs of Blurt Master Constable; notes that they are meant to be accompanied (although music survives for only two), which is more usual in private theatre plays.

503 Salingar, L.G. "The Revenger's Tragedy and the Morality Tradition." Scrutiny 6 (1938): 402-24. A discussion of the themes and morality structure of the play; assumes Tourneur as author. Final comments argue that his plays do not achieve a "dramatic reorientation"; moreover, he adds, the only dramatist other than Shakespeare to achieve "such a reorientation" was Middleton. (This essay is reprinted in Elizabethan Drama, pp. 208-224.)

504 ----------. "The Revenger's Tragedy: Some Possible Sources." MLR 60 (1965): 3-12. A discussion of various possible sources of material in the play; concludes that it was a satire-tragedy drawn from historical reading and contemporary influences, and therefore composed by a method unusual in an era when most plays followed one general story.

505 Salingar, Leo. "The Changeling and the Drama of Domestic Life." E&S (n.s.) 32 (1979): 80-96. Argues that Changeling's limitations, as well as its "special kind of intensity," come from its "concentration upon domestic life"; it is a "penetrating analysis of a social myth," in which Beatrice is led astray by her confidence in her social status, but this emphasis on "criticism" of social morality lessens the effect of the tragedy.

506 Sargent, Roussel. "Theme and Structure in Middleton's A Game At Chess." MLR 66 (1971): 721-30. A discussion of the play that goes beyond the political allegory; notes the elements of the morality tradition and finds that the play illustrates "aggressive evil attacking guileless innocence" and yet suffering defeat.

507 Schoenbaum, Samuel. "Blurt, Master Constable: A Possible Authorship Clue." Renaissance News 13 (1960): 7-9. Discusses a clue to the authorship of Blurt in a scene from Wily Beguiled (xiii.1661-4), which apparently refers to Dekker.

508 ----------. "A Chaste Maid in Cheapside and Middleton's City Comedy." In Holzknecht, pp. 287-309. An extensive discussion of Chaste Maid; argues that "the harshness of [the play]--its essential misanthropy--prefigures the somber tragicomedies and tragedies to follow", although the mood is "Rabelaisian as well as sardonic, and great gales of laughter sweep through the play." Notes Middleton's contemporary reference, "realistic comedy," and irony.

509 ----------. "Hengist, King of Kent and Sexual Preoccupation in Jacobean Drama." PQ 29 (1950): 182-98. Discusses the Jacobean drama's "singular interest in problems of sexual transgression" and Middleton's "interest in sin and the consequences of sin"; contrasts Hengist with chronicle history plays. Notes that the play was termed a comedy on the title page of its first quarto; the subplot concerning the Mayor of Quinborough was considered the main plot for many years.

510 ----------. "Middleton's Share in The Honest Whore, Part I and II." NQ 197 (1952): 3-4. Attributes most of Honest Whore (and Blurt) to Dekker; concludes that the play "cannot be regarded as part of the Middleton canon."

511 ----------. "Middleton's Tragicomedies." MP 54 (1956), 7-19. Discusses in depth The Witch, The Old Law, More Dissemblers Besides Women and A Fair Quarrel; considers the role of Middleton's collaborators in these plays. Emphasises Middleton's "conception of a mercilessly just universe" and his irony as elements continued in his tragedies; concludes that the plays show "the intellectual passion which led [Middleton] to envision the ironic order that gives coherence to his individual works and continuity to his ... productivity.

512 ----------. "A New Middleton Record." MLR 55 (1960): 82-84. Notes some evidence of Middleton's financial precariousness in court records of 1611 and 1612; suggests that civic employment finally helped his situation.

513 ----------. "The Revenger's Tragedy and Middleton's Moral Outlook." NQ 196 (1951): 8-10. Discusses Middleton's view of sin ("he sees sin as blind, sinners as groping through a universe they cannot understand, unaware that the universe has a moral order ... [becoming] their own agents of retribution") and connects it with the viewpoint of Revenger's Tragedy.

514 ----------. "The Revenger's Tragedy: A Neglected Source." NQ 195 (1950): 338. Suggests as a source, with reference to nineteenth-century commentators, Varchi's Storia Fiorentina, in one version or another.

515 ----------. "The Revenger's Tragedy: Jacobean Dance of Death." MLQ 15 (1954): 201-7. Discusses the later medieval "danse macabre" and its re-emergence in the Jacobean era; notes its influences in Revenger's Tragedy and concludes that the "danse" and the play provide "a timeless parable of man's wickedness and God's punishment for sin."

516 Scott-Kilvert, Ian. "Thomas Middleton." Nine #5 (Autumn 1950): 315-327. Notes Middleton's "photographic presentation of London life"; discusses Chaste Maid and argues that "the implication in this play is that Middleton regarded human folly as incurable." Observes that Middleton used imagery "to illustrate a particular state of mind."

517 Seaton, Ethel. "Richard Galis and the Witches of Windsor." Library (series 4) 18 (1937): 268-78. Provides an explanation of a phrase in The Old Law (V.i.) involving William Dickens.

518 Shaaber, M.A. "The Ant and the Nightingale and Father Hubburds Tale." University of Pennsylvania Library Chronicle 13.2 (1947): 13-16. Suggests that the edition numbered 17881 in the Short Title Catalogue is really the first edition, while the edition marked 17880 is the second, because the latter has an extra tale. (See Price, 473, for a discussion of the same evidence, but with different conclusions about the reason for the confusion.)

519 Shand, G.B. "The Elizabethan Aim of The Wisdom of Solomon Paraphrased." In "Accompaninge the players", pp. 67-77. An attempt to "attach a critical handle to isolated stretches" of a poem that is a "stupefying read." Notes the poem's "patriotic protestantism" and its Calvinistic tinge, but wonders why Middleton made it "so long."

520 ----------. "The Naming of Sir Walter Whorehound." NQ 226 (1982): 136-7. Discusses the various meanings and pronunciations of the name of "one of [Middleton's] more distasteful comic figures." Notes the vegetative meaning for "horehound" and comments upon the "multiple facets of the character" shown in his name.

521 ----------. "The Two Editions of Thomas Middleton's The Blacke Booke." PBSA 71 (1977): 325-28. Notes the two distinct quartos of the pamphlet published in 1604, the second "a rather inattentive line-by-line resetting of Q1."

522 Sherman, Jane. "The Pawn's Allegory in Middleton's A Game at Chesse." RES (n.s.) 29 (1978): 147-159. Discusses Middleton's "tight, hard caricature of current affairs," focussing on the pawns' plots as a political allegory--an "'estates drama'"--and as a mirror of the story of the main plot. Emphasises Middleton's detachment.

523 Simmons, J.L. "Diabolical Realism in Middleton and Rowley's The Changeling." RenD (n.s.) 11 (1980): 135-70. A study of the Jacobean approaches to psychology as seen in Changeling. Notes that Beatrice perceives everything in a sexual way, including damnation; argues that the Essex divorce case and the Overbury murder trial were sources for Beatrice's character and Diaphanta's role. Concludes that the "psychology" of the play involves surrender to the devil; Beatrice and De Flores become "literal demon lovers."

524 Simpson, Percy. "Thomas Middleton's Women Beware Women." MLR 33 (1938): 45-6. A clarification of four cruxes that confused Dyce and Bullen: I.ii.46-9, I.ii.54-8, II.i.58-60 and III.i.176-7.

525 Slights, William W.E. "The Trickster-Hero and Middleton's _A Mad World, My Masters_." _Comparative Drama_ 3 (1969): 87-98. Considers the origins of the trickster-hero: the Vice of the morality tradition and the _adulescens_ and witty slave of Roman comedy. Finds Middleton's comedy focussed towards the festive ending, owing "much of its exuberance to the absence of convincing psychological motivation"; concludes that _Mad World_ is "a parody of the moral view expressed in such dramatic satires as those of Jonson ... Middleton conspicuously thumbs his nose at moral posturing when he asserts that the world muddles through in its madcap way. But his emphasis is disturbing ... finally closer to cynicism than anything we find in Jonson's most bitter vituperations, for it counts all human efforts as nothing." Although a minority view, a persuasive and thoughtful counter to the "moral psychology" critics.

526 Soens, Adolph L. "Lawyers, Collusions and Cudgels: Middleton's _Anything for a Quiet Life_ I.i.220-221." _ELN_ 7 (1969): 248-54. Discusses the simile comparing lawyers to fencers, with reference to contemporary events and the complexities of the comparison.

527 Southall, R. "A Missing Source-Book for Middleton's _A Game at Chesse_." _NQ_ 207 (1962): 145-46. Discusses the need to find a source for the fishpond/infants story in V.iii, a story referred to in a Sampson Price sermon (1613) that misses details given in the play; notes the origin of the story in a medieval text and posits the existance of a Renaissance edition or version that would have been a common source for Middleton and Price. (See Pineas, 462, for reaction and Yachnin, 575, for further discussion.)

528 Spencer, Theodore. "The Elizabethan Malcontent." In _Joseph Quincy Adams Memorial Studies_, pp. 523-35. A study of the "general gloom and discontent" around the court after 1595 and its reflection in the dramatic "malcontent"; examines the five basic types of melancholiacs.

529 Stafford, T.J. "Middleton's Debt to Chaucer in _The Changeling_." _Bulletin of the Rocky Mountain Modern Language Association_ 22 (1968): 208-13. (**_Popular School_)

530 Sternlicht, Sanford. "Tourneur's Imagery and _The Revenger's Tragedy_." _PLL_ 6 (1970): 192-97. Summarises the authorship controversy; studies the imagery of _Revenger's Tragedy_ and _Atheist's Tragedy_, using "statistical comparisons" and referring to Ellis-Fermor's image patterns (see 261); concludes that the images in each play are quite different from those in the other and "there seems little reason to continue to insist on acscribing _The Revenger's Tragedy_ to Tourneur."

531 Stoll, Elmer E. "Heroes and Villains: Shakespeare, Middleton, Byron, Dickens." RES 18 (1942): 257-69. Discusses the dramaturgical effects ("dramaturgy, not realism") that compel audience response, in spite of weaknesses in character development; discusses The Changeling III.iv.

532 Stonex, Arthur Bivens. "The Usurer in Elizabethan Drama." PMLA 31 (1916): 190-210. Discusses the dramatic history and the different presentations of the usurer in Elizabethan-Jacobean drama; mentions A Trick to Catch the Old One, with its two usurers.

533 Strauss, Jennifer. ""Dance in Thomas Middleton's Women Beware Women." Parergon 29 (1981): 37-43. (**MLA Bibliography 1982)

534 Sullivan, Frank. "Macbeth, Middleton's Witch, and Macbeth Again." Los Angeles Tidings 24 September 1948: 6. Gives the date for The Witch as 1609. (**Popular School)

535 ----------. "Swathie." TLS 24 June 1939: 373. Notes that "swathie" in The Witch I.i.61-2 should be "froathie," "Liard" in V.ii.66 should be "liand," and "creature" in V.ii.17 should be "Greatness."

536 Sutherland, James R. "Cyril Tourneur." TLS 16 Apr. 1931: 307. A biographical note on Tourneur (the only article on Tourneur during 1930 and 1931 in TLS that does not concern Revenger's Tragedy).

537 Sykes, H. Dugdale. "Thomas Middleton's Early Non-Dramatic Works." NQ 148 (1925): 435-438. A study of Middleton's early poetry and prose, with a discussion of authorship questions that demonstrates Middleton's authorship (no longer in dispute now that his birthdate has been established as 1580 and these are seen as juvenilia).

538 ----------. "A Webster-Middleton Play: Anything for a Quiet Life." NQ 141 (1921): 181-3, 202-4, 225-6, with corrections 300. Argues for Webster's authorship of the main plot and divides the play's authorship scene by scene; in NQ 142 (1922): 50, he responds to Oliphant's reaction to his series of articles (see 442) and agrees that he may have over-estimated Webster's contribution.

539 Szenczi, N.I. "The Tragi-Comedies of Middleton and Rowley." In Studies in English Philology: Essays Presented ... to Prof. A.B. Yolland. Dept. of English, Royal Hungarian Pazmany Peter University of Sciences, 1937. Vol. 2. (**Popular School)

540 Tannenbaum, Samuel A. "A Middleton Forgery." PQ 12 (1933): 33-36. Suggests Middleton's "petition" about Game at Chess is a forgery and the actors were not imprisoned when the play was censored. (For a disagreement, see Wagner, 552; for another mention, see Bullough, 207.)

541 Taylor, Arnold C. TLS 1 Jan. 1931: 12. A note, referring to the Nicoll edition of The Revenger's Tragedy, about "bewitching" and "bewildering" as used in the play and in the edition.

542 Taylor, Archer. "Proverbs and Proverbial Phrases in the Plays of Thomas Middleton." San Francisco Quarterly 23 (1959): 79-89. Gives a useful reference glossary of phrases; uses the outdated 1570 birthdate for Middleton.

543 Taylor, J. Chesley. "Metaphors of the Moral World: Structure in The Changeling." Tulane Studies in English 20 (1972): 41-56. Discusses the play's "unifying concept" of transformation, its imagery and Renaissance background; argues that "the changes which the characters undergo are essentially moral changes."

544 Taylor, Michael. "Realism and Morality in Middleton's A Mad World, My Masters." Literature and Psychology 18 (1968): 166-78. Discusses the way in which Middleton's dramatic world is "a distortion and conventionalising" of the "real" world; argues that the moral concerns in Middleton's plays are not well integrated, although he maintained "a constant, if often detached, preoccupation with such moral questions as sin, guilt and remorse."

545 Teagarden, Lucetta J. "The Dekker-Middleton Problem in Michaelmas Term." Texas Studies in English 26 (1947): 49-58. Finds evidence of a continuing relationship between Middleton and Dekker from 1602 to 1611; argues that the gulling scenes in Michaelmas Term (1607) may come from Dekker's Lanthorne and Candlelight (1608), seen in manuscript by his collaborator Middleton.

546 Treglown, Jeremy. "A Fair Quarrel." Plays and Players 26.7 (April 1979): 21 and 23. A review of the National Theatre production of the play, directed by William Gaskill. Notes the psychological analysis of Captain Ager and the parallel plots; finds the roaring scenes (much to his surprise) funny.

547 Turner, Robert K., Jr. "Dekker's 'Back-Door'd Italian': I Honest Whore, II.i.355." NQ 205 (1960): 25-6. Argues that "back door'd" refers to anal intercourse. (See Levin, 378, for further references.)

548 ----------. "Act-End Notations in Some Elizabethan Plays." MP 72 (1975): 238-47. An examination of the kind of copy with which act-end notations are associated (as part of an discussion of the copy for Twelfth Night in the First Folio). Discusses Middleton's The Witch and A Game at Chess manuscripts, and the printed text of Michaelmas Term (1607) and A Mad World, My Masters (1908); notes the difference between texts with theatrical associations (e.g. prompt copies) and those without (e.g. authorial copies, etc.).

549 Ure, Peter. "Patient Madman and Honest Whore: The Middleton-Dekker Oxymoron." E&S 19 (1966): 18-40. Discusses the "patient" men in Phoenix, Honest Whore (esp. Part I) and Anything for a Quiet Life; argues that Middleton and Dekker (and especially Middleton) were illustrating the "ethic" of patience, which "presumably holds that if you endure long and suffer even the worst wrongs meekly your persecutors will turn from their wickedness and permit you to live." Comments as well on the Dekker-Middleton collaboration and the responsibility of each for theme and character development. (Essay is reprinted in Collected Essays on Jacobean Drama by Peter Ure, ed. J.C. Maxwell; see 119.)

550 Wadsworth, Frank W. "The Revenger's Tragedy." MLR 50 (1955): 307. Discusses the revenge elements of Atheist's Tragedy and Revenger's Tragedy; suggests that the Revenger's Tragedy, like the Atheist's, "rejects all but the view that God will revenge", and thus supports the Tourneur ascription. (Agrees with Foakes, 274, and Adams, 155.)

551 Wagner, Bernard M. "Cyril Tourneur." TLS 23 Apr. 1931: 327. Various notes on the Tourneur "canon," including one Revenger's Tragedy trait that is more like Middleton's work than Tourneur's other work.

552 ----------. "A Middleton Forgery." PQ 14 (1935): 287-88. A response to Tannenbaum's suggestion (540); notes that the petition in question (about A Game at Chess) is "a genuine composition contemporary with the play," as copies appear in early seventeenth-century poetry miscellanies.

553 ----------. "New Allusions to A Game at Chesse." PMLA 44 (1929): 827-34. A collection of contemporary references to the play from private correspondence and legal warrants; notes the play's "phenomenal" earnings.

554 Waith, Eugene M. "The Ascription of Speeches in The Revenger's Tragedy." MLN 57 (1942): 119-21. Rearranges the speech divisions in one place each in V.i and V.iii.

555 Wells, William. "Timon of Athens." NQ 138 (1920): 266-69. Discusses the case for Middleton's hand in the "non-Shakespearean" parts of Timon; the first major suggestion of Middleton's involvement (see also Lake, 147, for further discussion).

556 Wharton, T.F. "'Yet I'll Venture': Moral Experiment in Early Jacobean Drama." In Jacobean Drama Studies 95: 3-17. Salzburg, 1980. A comparison of Shakespeare's "moral dividing-line" decisions with the Jacobean sense of moral "unreality," with reference to The Changeling (Alsemero's fidelity test) and Women Beware Women's mood of isolation.

557 White, Martin. "The Changeling." Plays and Players 26.4 (January 1979): 13. A review of the Aldwych production, directed by Terry Hands; notes the extreme overt sexuality of the production and its effect (see Scott, 100, for further discussion of this production).

558 Wigler, Stephen. "If Looks Could Kill: Fathers and Sons in The Revenger's Tragedy." A discussion of eye images and their sexual connections; argues that the play's conception of sexuality is "a reaction to, and an effort to cope with, a powerful and relatively unelaborated Oedipal fantasy." Notes Vindice's obsession with incest and finds the grotesque comedy of the play part of its frightening quality: "The Revenger's Tragedy resolutely inhabits and obeys the laws of the grotesque cosmos of the human unconscious." Accepts and refers to Middleton as author of the play.

559 ---------. "Parent and Child: The Pattern of Love in *Women Beware Women*." In "*Accompaninge the players*", pp. 183-201. Argues that "the pattern of love in *Women Beware Women* is "ultimately something very close to incest"; details the various relationships in the play and points out how all resemble parent-child relationships (except Bianca and Leantio), with both Bianca and Isabella looking for protective fathers and Livia appearing an "incestuous mother" with, first, Hippolyto and second, Leantio.

560 ----------. "Penitent Brothel Reconsidered: The Place of the Grotesque in Middleton's *A Mad World, My Masters*." *Literature and Psychology* 25 (1975): 17-26. Defines the grotesque as "a mixture of styles which produces feelings of bemusement and perhaps of anxiety" in the reader or audience; compares Middleton to Bruegel in the way both undermine their audience's expectations, turning ordinary things into unexpectedly grotesque images. Gives Penitent a Freudian explanation.

561 ----------. "Thomas Middleton's *A Chaste Maid in Cheapside*: The Delicious and the Disgusting." *American Imago* 33 (1976): 197-215. Suggests that the "distasteful" reaction to the play is deliberately provoked by Middleton; the play is "comic-grotesque" rather than merely comic. Analyses the play from a psychoanalytic viewpoint; argues that "the sources of the ambivalent response to *A Chaste Maid* include the infantile oral and phallic ambivalence which Middleton's grotesquery makes us re-experience."

562 Williams, Robert I. "Machiavelli's *Mandragola*, Touchwood Senior, and the Comedy of Middleton's *A Chaste Maid in Cheapside*." *SEL* 10 (1970): 385-96. Discusses the possible influence of *Mandragola* on the characterisation of Touchwood Senior; argues that Middleton's "moral ambiguity" results in "comedy of anguish ... stemming from faith in a tender heart and, at the same time, from recognition that a tender heart is powerless in this world, unless ... partially corrupt."

563 Williams, Gordon. "A Sample of Elizabethan Sexual Periphrasis." *Trivium* 3 (1968): 94-100. (***Popular School*)

564 Williams, Gwyn. "The Cuckoo, the Welsh Ambassador." *MLR* 51 (1956): 223-25. An examination of the meaning of the word "lidger" (resident ambassador) in *Your Five Gallants* V.i. and of the identification of the cuckoo as the "Welsh Ambassador."

565 Williams, Sheila. "Two Seventeenth Century Semi-Dramatic Allegories of Truth the Daughter of Time." Guildhall Miscellany 2 (1963): 207-20. Discusses The Triumphs of Truth (1613); Middleton produced "a form ... closely allied to the ... Morality Play."

566 Williamson, Marilyn L. "Blurt, Master Constable III.iii and The Batchelars Banquet." NQ 202 (1957): 519-21. Notes a possible relationship between the two; argues that "the author of Blurt had access to a copy of The Batchelars Banquet before it was published" and therefore suggests that the relationship between the author of the play, the pamphlet, and Middleton and Dekker needs examination. (Later critics have given Dekker Blurt but taken away Banquet; see also Teagarden, 595, and Ure, 549, for Dekker-Middleton interchanges.)

567 ----------. "Middleton's Workmanship and the Authorship of The Puritan." NQ 202 (1957): 50-1. Argues for the Middleton attribution (frequently accepted; see Lake, 147); notes that the play's "combination of religious satire and the comedy of sex" resembles Family of Love.

568 ----------. "The Phoenix: Middleton's Comedy de Regimine Principum." Renaissance News 10 (1957): 183-7. Discusses the relationship between Occleve's De Regimine Principum and "the most sententious and didactic of all Thomas Middleton's plays"; argues that the play was meant to be presented to James. (See Bawcutt--178, Power--466-467, and Dodson--238--for more discussion of this idea.)

569 Wilson, Edward M. and Olga Turner. "The Spanish Protest against A Game at Chess." MLR 44 (1949): 476-82. Discusses the reports of the Spanish Ambassador, Don Carlos Coloma, on the characters and staging of Chess; quotes from a letter, dated August 1624, describing the play's popularity. (For more from Don Carlos, see Phialas, 460.)

570 Wilson, F.P. "Ralph Crane, Scrivener to the King's Players." Library (series 4) 7 (1926): 194-215. Discusses manuscripts by Crane, including The Witch (MS Malone 12) and two manuscripts of A Game at Chess (Lansdowne 690 and MS Malone 25); includes plates with facsimiles from each manuscript giving samples of Crane's writing.

571 Withington, Robert. "The Lord Mayor's Show for 1623." *PMLA* 30 (1915): 110-115. Notes the descriptions of the show, including Middleton's *Triumphs of Integrity*; suggests that Munday was Middleton's collaborator, doing the "festivities on the water" while Middleton organised those on land.

572 Wright, Louis B. "A Game at Chess." *TLS* 16 February 1928: 112. Argues that the play was sponsored by Charles and Buckingham and was "conscious political propaganda for the policy of intervention in the Palatinate." (For an argument, see Bald, 170.)

573 ----------. "Social Aspects of Some Belated Moralities." *Anglia* 54 (1930): 107-48. A discussion and summary of the major late sixteenth-century and early seventeenth-century manifestations of the morality play; an invaluable guide to the plays Middleton may have used as sources and his audience would have known well.

574 Yachnin, Paul. "*A Game at Chess* and Chess Allegory. *SEL* 22 (1982): 317-30. Argues that Middleton used literary "chess allegory" rather than his own knowledge of chess in *Game at Chess* and in the chess scene in *Women Beware Women*; suggests sources for some of the allegorical points, including Rabelais. Argues that Middleton "exploited a conventional homiletic mode" and was "demonstrably indifferent towards technical precision."

575 ----------. "A New Source for Middleton's *A Game at Chess*." *NQ* 225 (1980): 157-8. Notes that Foxe's *Acts and Monuments* gives all the details of the "fishpond and dead children" example. (See, for earlier discussions, Southall--527--and Pineas--462.)

576 Zimmerman, Susan. "The Folger Manuscripts of Thomas Middleton's *A Game at Chesse*: A Study in the Geneology of Texts." A study and collation of the nine extant texts of the play; argues that evidence from the Folger manuscripts "establishes a new hierarchy of authoritative texts and a new basis for a critical edition of the play." Argues throughout with Bald's established hierarchy of *Chess* texts (see 168, 172 and his edition of the play, 606).

Part Three: Primary Sources

Collected Works

577 Brooke, C.F. Tucker, ed. *The Shakespeare Apocrypha*. Oxford: Clarendon, 1929 (first published 1908). A collection of the anonymous plays loosely associated with Shakespeare's name; several have been attributed to Middleton. Contains *The Puritan* (pp. 219-248), a play of Puritan satire and city comedy double plots; play is dated c. 1607. Also contains *A Yorkshire Tragedy*, attributed by some to Middleton.

578 Bullen, A.H., ed. *The Works of Thomas Middleton*. New York: AMS Press, 1964 (first published 1885-6). 8 vols.; includes pageants and early poetry and prose. This edition remains the most recent complete edition, but is generally available only in the reprint form, and has been largely superseded by single editions of most of the major works in the canon. The introduction speaks of Middleton's amusing comedies and "blood-tingling" tragedies.

579 Dyce, Rev. Alexander, ed. *The Works of Thomas Middleton*. London: Lumley, 1840. The standard edition of Middleton's works, now nearly 150 years old, is still referred to by modern editors. Bullen's edition, not always accessible, is based quite closely on Dyce's; most modern textual arguments involve Dyce's edition in some way. Contains the same contents as Bullen, although Bullen adds some additional pageants and prose works.

580 Ellis, Havelock, ed. *The Best Plays of the Old Dramatists: Thomas Middleton*, introduced by Algernon Charles Swinburne (the Old Mermaids series). London: Vizetelly, 1887 (reprinted by Scholarly Press). 2 vols. Volume 1 includes the Swinburne introduction, a brief biography (now inaccurate), and editions of *A Trick to Catch the Old One*, *The Changeling*, *A Chaste Maid in Cheapside*, *Women Beware Women* and *The Spanish Gipsy*, and volume 2, *The Roaring Girl*, *The Witch*, *A Fair Quarrel*, *The Mayor of Quinborough* (*Hengist, King of Kent* in most recent criticism) and *The Widow*. Ellis collated Dyce and Bullen for his edition; the text is in modernised spelling, with no notes.

Swinburne's introductory essay is a reprint of an article on Middleton in *Nineteenth Century* (Jan. 1886) and is reprinted again in *The Age of Shakespeare* (1908); for some presumed notes on it, see Larsen, 399. Swinburne admired the "sunny" world of *The Widow*.

581 Frost, David L., ed. The Selected Plays of Thomas Middleton. Cambridge: Cambridge University Press, 1978. Includes A Mad World, My Masters, A Chaste Maid in Cheapside, Women Beware Women, and The Changeling, as well as a bibliography of Middleton's works, including conjectural ones. The introduction is a general survey, largely "factual and historical", with traditional critical positions (some plays are moral, some not), although Frost finds overall a "disturbing fascination with oddities of vice." A modernised text, with light notes.

> Reviewed, in MP 78 (1980): 172-5, by Caroline Asp, who gives the edition a thorough discussion and finds it "a handsome volume," but recommends instead the Revels editions, largely because "the critical material is outmoded in its method and misleading in its premises."
>
> Also reviewed, in YES 11 (1981): 245-47, by Peter Hollindale, who notes that the series gives little scope for critical comment and that Frost distorts Middleton in emphasising his "cynicism and pessimism." Finds the edition effective, although "not free of error."
>
> Also reviewed, in RES 30 (1979): 348-50, by Gary Taylor, who comments that he "cannot honestly recommend" the edition, as the editor is defeated by "the format or planning of the series [Plays by Renaissance and Restoration Dramatists, Cambridge University Press] and the bibliographical material is "not always accurate."

582 Gayley, Charles Mills, ed. The Later Contemporaries of Shakespeare: Fletcher and Others. Vol. 3 of A Comparative View of the Fellows and Followers of Shakespeare in Comedy (Part Two). New York: Macmillan, 1937. A collection and commentary that includes an edition by H. Butler Clarke of The Spanish Gipsy (pp. 105-203; sometimes attributed, in whole or in part, to Ford; see Lake, 147; Clarke gives Middleton and Rowley as authors). The introduction by Gayley, "Part Nine, Popular Comedy to 1614: Middleton and Contemporary Manners" (pp. xx-xxv), gives a typical negative view of Middleton; he shows "vulgarity and ... moral obtuseness" even in his best comedy.

583 Gomme, Andor H., ed. Jacobean Tragedies. London: Oxford University Press, 1969. Contains The Changeling (pp. 239-306), The Revenger's Tragedy (pp. 77-155) and Women Beware Women (pp. 156-238). Texts are modernised spelling, with notes; the introduction comments that The Changeling and Women Beware Women "have some claim to be considered the most powerful plays written in English since the death of Shakespeare."

> Reviewed in NQ 215 (1970): 232-33 by J.C. Maxwell, who finds it a "capable annotated edition of five important tragedies" with a "serviceable" introduction; makes a few emendations in notes on Revenger's Tragedy, Changeling, and Women Beware Women.

584 Lawrence, Robert G., ed. Jacobean and Caroline Comedies. London: Dent, 1973. Contains an edition of A Trick to Catch the Old One (pp. 1-72), in modern spelling with light notes; the brief introduction speaks of the play's "basic theme of corruption."

585 ----------. ed. Jacobean and Caroline Tragedies. London: Dent, 1975. Contains a modern-spelling edition of Women Beware Women, with light notes and an introduction discussing the sources and conventions used in the play. A brief general introduction calls the final act "disappointing," while the play's introduction speaks of "apparent inconsistencies of character."

586 Muir, Kenneth, ed. Three Plays. London: Dent, 1975. Contains A Chaste Maid in Cheapside, Women Beware Women, and The Changeling. The introduction comments that most critics now regard Middleton as "the best of Shakespeare's successors," and argues that he is not cynical but rather has "an acceptance of the fallen state of man." The text has modernised spelling, with light notes and a glossary.

> Reviewed in SCN 35 (1977): 118-19 by Tinsley Helton, who comments that he can "see no justification for editions" such as this one, as it seems to serve no special purpose and contains plays of which several editions are already available.

587 Ornstein, Robert and Hazelton Spencer, eds. Elizabethan and Jacobean Tragedy: an Anthology. Boston: D.C. Heath, 1964. Contains a modern-spelling edition of The Changeling (pp. 173-208), with some notes. No appreciation of the subplot; the main plot is "the height" of Middleton's powers.

588 Price, George R., ed. Michaelmas Term and A Trick to Catch the Old One: A Critical Edition, ed. George R. Price. The Hague and Paris: Mouton, 1976 (Studies in English Literature, Vol. 91). (An old-spelling edition--see detailed notes under the individual plays, 613 and 627.) Considers these plays "Middleton's two best comedies."

589 Sampson, Martin W., ed. Thomas Middleton. New York: American Book Company, 1915. Contains editions of Michaelmas Term, A Trick to Catch The Old One, A Fair Quarrel, and The Changeling. Texts are modern spelling, with explanatory notes and a glossary at the end.

590 Tatlock, J.S.P. and R.G. Martin, eds. Representative English Plays from the Miracle Plays to Pinero. New York: Appleton-Century-Crofts, 1938 (second edition revised and altered). Includes a modern-spelling edition of The Changeling, pp. 383-419.

591 Wine, M.L., ed. Drama of the English Renaissance. New York: Modern Library, 1969. Contains a modernised edition of The Changeling, pp. 601-663, with glosses and explanatory notes. Finds the play "more like a study of sin than a tragedy of sinners"; Middleton is "clinical."

Editions of Individual Plays, in chronological order by play. Collaborator(s) and alternate attributions are noted in parentheses.

Blurt, Master Constable (Dekker?)

592 Ed. Thomas Leland Berger. Salzburg, 1979. A "critical, old-spelling edition"; gives Dekker as author on title page and discusses the authorship extensively in the introduction, concluding that the overwhelming evidence is in Dekker's favour. (See Holmes, 145 and 318, for the strongest argument against this attribution.)

The Changeling (with William Rowley)

(Much of the critical comment in editions of The Changeling has been devoted to a defence of or attack on the subplot and Rowley's contribution to the play. The annotations on the different editions indicate, when appropriate, each editor's approach to this discussion.)

593 Ed. N.W. Bawcutt. London: Methuen, 1958. Dates the play at 1622; notes that it was performed at court 4 January 1623/4. Describes the play as "a study in sin and retribution, expressed in terms of sexual relationships"; finds that the "moral order is finally re-established" in both main and sub-plot. The most frequently cited edition of the play. The text is modern spelling, with extensive notes, glosses, textual variants and an appendix on sources.

> Reviewed, in Zeitschrift fur Anglistik und Amerikanistik (Leipzig) 23 (1975): 68-70 [in German], by Jutta Schlosser.

594 Ed. Patricia Thomson. London: Ernest Benn, 1964. Comments that "there is no indication that [Beatrice-Joanna's] nature is unusually generously endowed"; Middleton's presentation of her shows a "disenchanged realism": she is "the wilful child of an imperious father." Finds the subplot neither "coherent nor appealing." Text is modernised, with running glosses and critical notes at the end.

595 Ed. Matthew W. Black. Philadelphia: University of Pennsylvania Press, 1966. The brief introduction mentions the "moral degeneration" of Beatrice-Joanna, defends the "artistic unity" of the two plots and finds a close collaboration between Middleton and Rowley; stage history and textual notes are also included. The text is modernised and revised in lineation and punctuation, with amplified and added stage directions and explanatory notes on each page.

596 Ed. Robert W. Corrigan, with an introduction by R.J. Kaufman. San Francisco: Chandler, 1966. An acting edition, with stage directions and a modernised text. The extensive introduction gives a psychological interpretation of the play, finding Middleton "nakedly clinical" in his presentation of "narrowly ritualized inner lives" in which sin becomes man's "tragic urge to self-reduction."

597 Ed. George W. Williams. Lincoln: University of Nebraska Press, 1966. Finds a close, successful collaboration in the play; the introduction discusses plot structure and image patterns, noting the play's "unifying concept of transformation," of appearance and reality as reflected in the image of the labyrinth and in madness. Dates the play at Spring 1622. Text has modernised spelling and punctuation, with explanatory notes.

598 _The Changeling 1653_ (Scolar Press Facsimile), with an introduction on play history, sources, and texts, by N.W. Bawcutt. Menston: Scolar Press, 1973.

A Chaste Maid in Cheapside

599 Ed. Alan Brissenden. London: Ernest Benn, 1968. The introduction discusses "Middleton's culminating achievement in comedy," a study of the corruption of money and sex in which Middleton "reverses normal values" to satirise "lust and sensuality." Finds Sir Walter's repentance a serious rejection of "the callous, inhuman world of the Allwits and Yellowhammers." Dates the play at 1611-1613, probably soon after Lent 1613. Text is modern spelling, with running notes and an appendix giving the ballad source (in Campion's _Art of Poesie_) for Allwit's speech, and a map of London.

600 Ed. Charles Barber. Edinburgh: Oliver and Boyd, 1969. The introduction focusses on the play's depiction of London city life, the "interplay of citizens and gentry" and the "capitalist market." Finds irony Middleton's only "mode of comment" in the play; considers Sir Walter's repentance farcical and part of the play's "exuberance." Dates the play at 1611-14, probably spring 1613. An old-spelling edition (with some regularisation), with text notes, notes on variant readings, and an extensive commentary.

601 Ed. R.B. Parker. London: Methuen, 1969. An extensive introduction discusses "the richest and most typical of Middleton's comedies," looks at structure and characterisation, and finds what Parker sees as Middleton's characteristic moral ambiguity, "farce stretched over moral discomfort." Dates the play at March-August 1613. Text is modern spelling, with extensive notes and appendices giving textual variants, performance details, music for the songs, and sources.

Reviewed in *Zeitschrift fur Anglistik und Amerikanistik* (Leipzig) 19 (1971): 314-16 [in German] by Jutta Schlosser.

602 *A Chaste Maid in Cheapside 1630* (Scolar Press Facsimile). Menston: Scolar Press, 1969.

A Fair Quarrel (with William Rowley)

603 Ed. R.V. Holdsworth. London: Ernest Benn, 1974. Finds "a collaboration as balanced, as close, and as sympathetic as ... *The Changeling*"; gives the main plot to Middleton and Act I and the subplot to Rowley. Considers the play an examination of "the nature of honour and the deceptiveness of reputation." Dates the play c. 1615-17. The text is modern spelling, with running notes and explanatory notes, and text information.

Reviewed in *RES* (n.s.) 27 (1976): 211-212 by Alan Brissenden, in a complimentary review that comments, "Middleton dealt with sex, money, and the darker intricacies of family relationships."

Also reviewed in *NQ* 221 (1976): 257-59 by J.C. Maxwell, who finds it "as full edition as most readers are ever likely to read" and makes some slight queries and emendations.

604 Ed. George R. Prince. Lincoln: University of Nebraska Press, 1976. Finds a close collaboration and makes an elaborate division of scene composition; considers the play's main theme the relationship between the various meanings of honour and morality. Dates the play at 1616-17. The text is modern spelling, with textual variants and explanatory notes, and appendices on the Roaring School and on additions to the play.

Reviewed in *NQ* 223 (1978): 80 by L.W. Conolly, who notes the useful appendix on the "roaring school" and the emphasis on textual and source materials.

Reviewed in SCN 36 (1978): 49-50 by Judd Arnold, who praises the notes on the protocol of the duel and the textual materials, notes that the introduction "avoids critical interpretation," and concludes that it is a "fine edition."

The Family of Love (with [or mainly?] Dekker?)

605 Ed. Simon Shepherd. (University of Nottingham Renaissance and Modern Studies.) Shepherd is sympathetic to Mrs. Purge; see further his Amazons and Warrior Women (102): "in this play, Mistress Purge is a victor; our supercilious grins must fade. It is her husband who is reprimanded ... The language of Puritanism allows her her freedom of sexual choice" (p. 61). (** Popular School, for edition citation only)

A Game at Chess

606 Ed. R.C. Bald. Cambridge: Cambridge University Press, 1929. Notes the dates of the play's performance, Friday 6 August to Monday 16 August 1624; comments that "few plays have ever caused such excitement in such a brief career" as Game at Chess. An old-spelling edition of the Trinity manuscript (in Middleton's hand), with additions from the Bridgewater-Huntingdon manuscript; an appendix gives letters showing reaction to the play. Heavy textual notes.

Reviewed in Library (series 4) 11 (1930): 105-16 by J. D[over] W[ilson], who finds it an "important edition of a highly important text," but comments on Bald's "perplexing" attitude towards printed texts, which Bald finds far inferior to the manuscripts. The review discusses extensively the political background to the play, and the printing and copying procedure.

607 Ed. J.W. Harper. London: Ernest Benn, 1966. The introduction emphasises Middleton's detachment and his "disillusioned view of life." Considers that the play has no psychological analysis--the chess pieces move according to rules, not motives and the play is written in "a form more closely akin to the masque than to the genres which were currently popular in the commercial theatre." Gives the dates of performance and discusses the public reaction. The text is in modern spelling, with textual notes and explanatory comments.

Reviewed in NQ 213 (1968): 276-79 by J.C. Maxwell, who finds the text "defective", with errors in transcription and in the textual and explanatory notes.

608 Ed. Milton Arthur Buettner. Salzburg, 1980. "A Textual Edition based on the manuscripts written by Ralph Crane." An extensive discussion of Crane's scribal characteristics; an old-spelling edition with textual variants listed.

Hengist, King of Kent: or The Mayor of Queenborough

609 Ed. R.C. Bald. New York: Scribner's, 1938. Notes the "mature verse" of the play and so dates it at 1616 to 1620, probably 1619-20; suggests a source in an earlier Valteger (1596). Describes the play as a "tragedy of ambition" which reflects the personal irony of the author's "own outlook on life." An old-spelling edition based on the Folger Shakespeare Library manuscript; extensive notes follow the text.

The Honest Whore, Part I (with Thomas Dekker)

610 The Dramatic Works of Thomas Dekker, ed. Fredson Bowers. Cambridge: Cambridge University Press, 1955. II.1-130. Although included in the standard Middleton editions, Dyce and Bullen, this is the most recent edition of the play; a certain amount of critical controversy exists over Middleton's share in the play, but most critics are inclined to give him a collaborator's share in Part I, although Bowers comments that "Middleton's part in the play seems to have been relatively minor." An old-spelling edition with textual variants and collation, and explanatory notes.

A Mad World, My Masters

611 Ed. Standish Henning. Lincoln: University of Nebraska Press, 1965. Discusses Middleton's realism--"local colour," simplified social detail, and "a seamy, depraved aspect of the world"; comments also on Middleton's irony--his amusement "is not, I think, to be understood as approval"--in what is "first and last a very funny play." Text is modern spelling, with explanatory notes and textual variants.

Michaelmas Term

612 Ed. Richard Levin. Lincoln: University of Nebraska Press, 1966. The introduction emphasises the realism and satire of the play, the "actual life of Jacobean London, vividly rendered by an accomplished satirist," and stresses the economic and class warfare elements, and the equation of money and sex in parallel plots. Text is modern spelling, with textual variants and explanatory notes.

613 Ed. George R. Price. The Hague and Paris: Mouton, 1976. An edition for "scholars and advanced students," with old-style spelling and punctuation only slightly changed. The brief introduction discusses authorship, date, sources, and text; explanatory and textual notes are appended.

No Wit, No Help Like a Woman's

614 Ed. Lowell E. Johnson. Lincoln: University of Nebraska Press, 1976. Finds the play not one of Middleton's best; argues that it is "a city comedy [whose] satiric blow is softened by the Fletcherian romance influence" and is therefore inferior to his early comedies. Considers the plot the chief weakness in the play; finds Weatherwise "a merry gull," one of Middleton's memorable characters. Dates the play at (probably) 1611. Text is modern spelling, with textual variants and explanatory notes.

The Old Law (with William Rowley)

615 Ed. Catherine M. Shaw. New York: Garland, 1982. An extensive introduction considers biographical information, date, collaboration attribution, performances, sources, staging, and text. An evaluative essay defends the play's structure as showing "three situations in which a man-made law leads to a violation of those moral laws set down in Holy Writ or ... morality leads to illegality," arguing that it is comedy, not tragi-comedy, and ends realistically, not romantically. The modernised text contains a running glossary with editorial notes; explanatory notes are appended.

The Phoenix

616 Ed. John Bradbury Brooks. New York: Garland, 1980. A "Critical, Modernised Edition"; the only modern edition of this play. Contains an extensive introduction that considers authorship (a lengthy discussion of possible collaboration by Dekker) and sources in detail, publication history, and editorial problems. Comments on Middleton's "originality" in the use of dramatic conventions. The play is annotated in detail, with both textual and commentary notes.

The Puritan

617 Ed. Sidney Heaven. The Puritaine or The Widow of Watling Street: a Comedy by an Unknown Author First Published in 1607 and Attributed, Falsely, to Shakespeare in the Third and Fourth Folio Editions of His Works, 1664-1685. London and Glasgow: Blackie, 1955 (The Garrick Playbooks). The introduction discusses staging, character, sources and historical background; the text is modern spelling, with textual and explanatory notes. No mention is made of Middleton as author.

618 Ed. Sylvia D. Feldman and G.R. Proudfoot. Oxford: Oxford University Press, 1973 (Malone Society Reprints).

The Revenger's Tragedy (Tourneur? Anon.?)

(The full list of editions of The Revenger's Tragedy is to be found in bibliographies on Cyril Tourneur--see Forker, 669, and Tucker, 679; both contain as well a complete discussion of the whole authorship controversy.)

To sum up the most recent individual editions: James L. Rosenberg (San Francisco: Chandler, 1962) ignores the question entirely, accepting Tourneur without discussion; Lawrence J. Ross (Lincoln: University of Nebraska Press, 1966) admits he "does not know" who wrote the play; R.A. Foakes (London: Methuen, 1966) leans towards Tourneur but prefers the "Anonymous" label; Brian Gibbons (London: Benn, 1967) chooses Tourneur; George Parfitt (in The Plays of Cyril Tourneur [Cambridge: Cambridge University Press, 1978]) prefers the "Anonymous" label, but includes the play in his collection; Jackson (1983; see below) chooses Middleton (although libraries shelve his edition under Tourneur anyway). I include the following edition in full because its title page makes a specific attribution to Middleton.

619 Ed. MacD[onald] P. Jackson. London and Toronto: Associated University Presses, 1983. A facsimile of the 1607/8 quarto; an extensive introduction surveys the text, sources, date and authorship question, arguing emphatically for Middleton (the title page is "The Revenger's Tragedy: Attributed to Thomas Middleton").

Reviewed in SEL 24 (1984): 405 by Richard P. Wheeler, who finds Jackson's evidence "persuasive," but notes the need for "critical substantiation" that can show "integral thematic connections" with Middleton's other plays, both comedy and tragedy.

The Roaring Girl (with Thomas Dekker)

620 Ed. Andor Gomme. London: Ernest Benn, 1976. A modernised text, with glosses and explanatory notes and an appendix on canting. The introduction finds the play a close collaboration, with the controlling hand Middleton's and Dekker's contribution the sentimentality. Argues that the play, one of "the splendid series of satiric comedies of London life," is less amoral than Middleton's other comedies; "virtue [is] victorious" and is also "seen to be delightful and vice ugly." Dates the play at 1607-8.

Reviewed, in NQ 223 (1978): 79-81, by L.W. Conolly, who calls the introduction "lucid and scholarly" and notes the difficulty of staging the play for a modern audience.

The Second Maiden's Tragedy (Anon.?)

621 Ed. W.W. Greg. London: Oxford University Press, 1909 (Malone Society Reprints). A reprint of MS Lansdowne 807 (British Museum), with an introduction on textual questions and play history and a note on scribal characteristics. With facsimile illustrations and running textual notes.

622 Ed. Anne Lancashire. Manchester: Manchester University Press, 1978 (completed in 1974). A detailed edition with modernised spelling. An extensive introduction considers textual, authorship, staging, and thematic matters; the text is thoroughly annotated as well. Notes the play's ironic and homiletic qualities, as well as its realistic and human ones; discusses in detail the authorship question and argues strongly for Middleton. (For further discussion of the play's homiletic qualities, see her essay, 366.)

Reviewed, in Cithara 18.2 (1979): 80-3, by Waldo F. McNeir. The reviewer gives a thorough discussion of the play and calls the edition "a fine edition of a mediocre Jacobean revenge tragedy."

Also reviewed, in SCN 37 (1979): 79-80, by Sara Jayne Steen, who calls the edition "worth the wait" and praises the "fully-documented annotation"; she wonders why all alternate readings were not noted so that readers could judge for themselves at points of discussion.

Also reviewed, in YES 11 (1981): 247-249, by M.L. Wine, who finds the play "superbly edited," with "careful transcription and extended commentary and annotation."

The Spanish Gipsy (with Rowley, and Ford? or just Ford?)

623 Ed. Edgar C. Morris. Belles Lettres Series, 1908 (** New Cambridge Bibliography).

A Trick to Catch the Old One

624 Ed. Charles Barber. Edinburgh: Oliver and Boyd, 1968. An old-spelling edition, with notes on the text, a commentary at the end of the play text, and glossary, and note on spellings. The introduction finds the play realistic, presenting "clearly and unsentimentally some of the social tensions of Jacobean England," the competition between citizen and gentleman, especially over money. Comments on Middleton's detachment and his irony; places Dampit outside the play, "a kind of symbol of the incoherence and rottenness of the usuring society depicted in the play." Dates the play at 1605-6.

625 Ed. G.J. Watson. London: Ernest Benn, 1968. A modernised edition, with running glosses and explanatory notes and a note on the text. The introduction argues that _Trick_ is "one of the most distinguished" of Middleton's plays; discusses at some length the satiric means by which Middleton suggests that "vice is normal ... the natural way of the world" and provides an "indirect moral commentary." Finds that Dampit provides a contrast that emphasises "the respectability of Lucre and Hoard"; notes Middleton's "colloquial, non-metaphoric" style. Dates the play at 1604-6, probably 1606.

626 _A Trick to Catch the Old One 1608_. Menston: Scolar Press, 1970. A Scolar Press facsimile; includes both "1608" title pages.

627 Ed. George R. Price. In his _Michaelmas Term and A Trick to Catch the Old One_. The Hague and Paris: Mouton, 1976. Pp. 127-227. A brief introduction considers date, publication and text, and sources; the text is intended "for the use of scholars and advanced students" and is old-spelling, with some regularisation of spelling and changes in punctuation. Light explanatory notes and notes on textual variants are appended.

The Widow

628 _A Critical Edition of Thomas Middleton's "The Widow"_, ed. Robert Trager Levine. Salzburg, 1975. A modern-spelling edition, with an extensive discussion of authorship, date, sources, stage history, and text; with explanatory notes and appendices on textual details. The introduction discusses the play's main themes, the way in which "greed for money subverts genuine love and friendship" and the stages of womanhood, and concludes that the play is like a city comedy and, although not among Middleton's best work, "entertaining." Dates the play at c. 1616; suggests Jonson and Fletcher as possible collaborators.

The Witch

629 Ed. L. Drees and Henry de Vocht. Louvain: Librairie Universitaire, 1945 (text completed 1938). An entirely textual edition, with an introduction on the history and form of the text and notes on textual variants. Modernised spelling.

630 Ed. W.W. Greg and F.P. Wilson. London: Oxford University Press, 1960 (reprint; first published 1948-50; Malone Society Reprints). A reprint of the manuscript, with textual notes; the introduction includes a discussion of the manuscript, the scribe (Ralph Crane), and the play's history.

Women Beware Women

631 Ed. Roma Gill. London: Ernest Benn, 1968. A modern-spelling edition with extensive running notes and glosses. The introduction discusses the play's concern with "the problems of wealth and the use of riches," particularly for citizen newly rich, and finds the play "cruel but oddly unmoving." Argues that the play's "unashamedly theatrical conclusion," in which "every punishment fit[s] its crime," emphasises Middleton's concern with moral judgement. Dates the play c. 1621.

632 Ed. Charles Barber. Edinburgh: Oliver and Boyd, 1969. An old-spelling edition, with textual notes, commentary and glossary. The introduction comments on the play's "observation of the real world, and remarkable psychological penetration," particularly in its examination of relationships between women and of the corruption "the desire for wealth" breeds. Finds "a complete detachment" on Middleton's part; the irony prevents audience sympathy and the characters are "blinded and doomed." Argues that the play's date is "wide open," ranging from 1613-14, or even earlier (because of a possible connection with The Revenger's Tragedy--a mid-career tragic phase for Middleton), to 1623-7.

633 Ed. J.R. Mulryne. London: Methuen, 1975. A modern-spelling edition, with running textual and explanatory notes, an extensive introduction, and appendices on sources and textual variants. The introduction comments on the way in which "characters contrive to forget their moral obligations"; the play shows "bleakly enough how completely this brings them to nothing." Argues that the play is initially a morality play, adding, "within the ordered framework," social realism. Finds Leantio and Livia the most effective characters. Surveys the play's various possible dates; suggest that c. 1621 is the most probable.

Reviewed, in Durham University Journal (n.s.) 38 (1976): 157-8, by N.W. Bawcutt, who finds that it "decisively supersedes all previous editions" with its "splendidly full commentary"; adds a few comments.

Reviewed, in RES (n.s.) 29 (1978): 88-93, by R.V. Holdsworth, who finds both merits (discussion of sources and dating) and defects (commentary, critical conclusion, textual editing) in the edition and recommends Roma Gill's edition.

Reviewed, in MLR 72 (1977): 897-99, by R.B. Parker, who lauds the thoroughness of the edition, especially in bibliography and source material, notes that it does not give an original interpretation, and finds the edition generally a good one.

Reviewed, in NQ 221 (1976): 261-63, by Roger Warren, who praises a "superb and sorely needed edition of a superb play"; finds the introduction "probably the best available criticism of the play" and adds only a few quibbles over punctuation and stage history.

Your Five Gallants

634 Ed. Clare Lee Colegrove. New York: Garland, 1979 (a published doctoral dissertation). An old-spelling edition with extensive textual notes, a bibliography, and 170 pages of explanatory notes. The introduction contains an essay on Middleton and on Your Five Gallants's audience, with a discussion of date, sources, and text; it emphasises Middleton's irony, which shows his "moral commitment" to social criticism even as he writes scenes of entertaining vice.

Editions of Non-Dramatic Works

635 The Ghost of Lucrece, ed. Joseph Quincy Adams. New York: Scribner's, 1937. Includes an introduction, a facsimile of the Folger copy and an edited text; the introduction discusses the Fortune's Wheel images of the poem and the position of the work in Middleton's canon (written before Eccles' research changed attitudes about Middleton's early work). Dates the composition of the poem at c. 1599.

636 Honourable Entertainments, ed. R.C. Bald and F.P. Wilson. Oxford: Oxford University Press, 1953 (Malone Society Reprint). An edited text of the 1621 edition of ten entertainments written for London civic events other than the October 29 pageants; probably published to mark Middleton's post as City Chronologer (granted 6 Sept. 1620).

637 The Inner Temple Masque or Masque of Heroes, ed. R.C. Bald. In A Book of Masques in Honour of Allardyce Nicoll, ed. T.J.B. Spencer and Stanley Wells. Cambridge: Cambridge University Press, 1967. Pp. 251-274. An edited version of the 1618 masque written for the New Year festivities. The introduction discusses the masque's performance and form; the text is modernised, with textual and explanatory notes. (For a review of this collection, see review of Ekeblad's contribution, 258.)

Part Four: Foreign-language studies

(Sources for unviewed items are given in parentheses following items, marked by **; the initial citation of a source gives the reference for full bibliographic information.)

Articles and Monographs

638 Abiteboul, Maurice. "Presence du baroque dans The Changeling." Baroque (1969) No. 4: 67-76. (**Cited in Gallenca, 279)

639 Aronstein, Philipp. Das englische Renaissancedrama. 1929. (**Popular School, 670)

640 Baxmann, E. Middletons Lustspiel: The Widow und Boccaccios Il Decamerone III.3 und II.2. Halle, 1904. (New Cambridge Bibliography, 680)

641 Bry, A. "Middleton et le public des 'city comedies.'" In Dramaturgie et societe, ed. Jean Jacquot. Paris, 1968. (**New Cambridge Bibliography and English Drama, 681) (See also Fuzier, 645.)

642 Christ, Karl. Quellenstudien zu den Dramen Thomas Middletons. Borna-Leipzig, 1905. A work frequently cited by critics. (**New Cambridge Bibliography)

643 Currie, Ryder Hector. "La Mysterieuse Initiation de William Rowley dans The Changeling." Revue Historique du Theatre 2 (1971): 156-70. (**Popular School Update, 670a)

644 Davril, Robert. Le Drame de John Ford. Paris: Didier, 1954. Argues that Ford learned from Middleton, possibly by collaborating with him; finds Middleton pessimistic, cynical, detached, and without humanity, a playwright who watches his characters destroy themselves.

645 Fuzier, Jean and Andre Bry. "The Changeling de Thomas Middleton et William Rowley: Bibliographie selective et critique." Bulletin de la Societe d'Etudes Anglo-Americaine de XVIIe et XVIIIe siecles 15 (1982): 7-33. (**MLA Bibliography (672) 1982)

646 ----------. "The Changeling et la tradition tragique elisabethaine: perversion ou subversion?" Etudes Anglaises (1983) No. 1: 1-10. (**Gallenca)

647 Grivelet, Michel. _Thomas Heywood et le drame domestique elisabethain_. 1957. (**_Popular School_)

648 Grossman, R. _Spanien und das elizabethanische Drama_. Hamburg, 1920. (**_New Cambridge Bibliography_)

649 Kawai, Mariko. "Game to shite no Sei: Thomas Middleton Ron." _Oberon_ (1982) 45: 94-106. (**_MLA Bibliography_ 1984)

650 Jacquot, Jean, ed. _La lieu theatral a la Renaissance_. Paris, 1964. Vol. 1. (**_Popular School_)

651 Jones-Davies, M.T. _Un peintre de la vie Londonienne_: Thomas Dekker. 1958. 2 vols. (**_Popular School_)

652 ----------, ed. _L'Or au temps de la Renaissance_: du mythe a l'economie. Paris: Bulletin du Centre de Recherches sur la Renaissance de l'Universite de Paris-Sorbonne, 1978.

> The collection is reviewed in _Cahiers Elisabethains_ 15 (April 1979): 114 by Jean Fuzier, who notes that the collection comprises twelve essays in French, including "Le Vocabulaire de l'or dans les appellations satiriques au temps de la Renaissance anglaise," by Marie-Madeleine Martinet (pp. 99-104), and "L'Or sur la scene elisabethaine: une aventure sociale," by M.T. Jones-Davies; overall he praises the collection for the "wealth and variety of the information it provides."

653 Jung, H. _Das Verhaltnis Middletons zu Shakspere_. Leipzig, 1904. (**_New Cambridge Bibliography_)

654 Maugeri, Aldo. _Studi su Thomas Dekker_. 1958. (**_Popular School_)

655 Rigaud, Nadia. "_The Changeling_: Aboutissement de la thematique middletonienne." _Bulletin de la Societe d'Etudes Anglo-Americaine de XVIIe et XVIII siecles_ 15 (1982): 69-85. Deals with love, choice, and murder. **_MLA Bibliography_ 1982))

656 Rigaud, N. "La Tolerance a l'egard des manquements a la chastete dans les pieces de Middleton." In _Tolerance et intolerances dans le monde anglo-americain aux XVIIe et XVIIIe siecles_. Nantes: Universite de Nantes, 1981. Pp. 99-112. Discussion of chastity in Middleton's plays. (**_MLA Bibliography_ 1982)

657 Rigaud, N.J. "Middleton analyste du pouvoir." In Le Pouvoir dans la litterature et la pensee anglaises, ed. N.J. Rigaud. Aix-en-Provence: Centre Aixois de Recherches Anglaises, Universite de Provence-Aix, 1981. Pp. 41-56. Discusses domestic and political power. (**MLA Bibliography 1982)

658 Rocca, Marinella. Una maschiaccia a Londra. Rome: Tipografia editrice dell'Orso. (**MHRA Bibliography (671) 1972)

659 Rocca Longa, Marinella. "Dalla satira comica alla commedia satirica nell'opera di Thomas Middleton." In Le forme del teatro, ed. Giorgio Melchiori. Rome: Ed. di Storia e Lett., 1979. Discusses satire and comedy. (**MLA Bibliography 1981)

660 Rolle, Dietrich. Ingenious structure: Die Dramatische Funktion der Sprache in der Tragodie der Shakespearezeit. Heidelberg: Carl Winter, 1971 (Anglistiche Forschungen, vol. 99).

Reviewed by E.A.J. Honigmann in NQ 218 (1973): 473-4, who describes the book as "an attempt to demonstrate 'how the major Jacobean playwrights managed to give artistic unity to their tragic plots.'" Finds it somewhat confused; questions the order of chapters and works cited and the use of terms and examples, but adds that Rolle's "incidental remarks can often stand on their own."

661 Sanbai, Ryuichi. "Changeling no Higeki no Sekai." In Susa Yasuo, Ogoshi Kazugo: Ryokyoju Taikan Kinen Ronbunshu. Kyoto: Apollonsha, 1980. Pp. 225-237. (**MLA Bibliography 1981)

662 Schlosser, Jutta. "Betrachtungen zu Middletons A Chaste Maid in Cheapside." Shakespeare Jahrbuch (Weimer) 117 (1981): 101-108.

663 ----------. "Zur Interpretation von Middletons The Changeling." Shakespeare Jahrbuch (Weimar) 111 (1975): 145-55.

664 Schoenbaum, Samuel. "Peut-on parler d'une "decadence" du theatre au temps des premier Stuarts?" In Dramaturgie et societe, ed. Jean Jacquot. Paris, 1968. (**English Drama)

665 Sedlak, Werner. Blankversveranderungen in Shakespeares spateren Tragodien: eine Interpretation von 'Othello,' 'King Lear,' 'Macbeth' und 'Antony and Cleopatra' (mit einem Ausblick auf J. Websters 'Duchess of Malfi' und Th. Middletons 'Women Beware Women' sowie einem Anhand zu 'Hamlet'). Munich: University of Munich, 1971. (Published doctoral dissertation.)

Reviewed, in Anglia 93 (1975): 522-25 [in German], by Hans-Jurgen Diller.

Editions of Plays

The following translations of The Changeling (most French versions emphasise the main plot) have appeared:

666 Les amants malefiques, ed. Georges Arout. L'Avant-Scene no. 362, 1966. (**Gallenca)

667 La Fausse Epouse, tragedie en quatre actes tiree de The Changeling de Thomas Middleton, trans. Paul Morand. Paris: Grasset, 1956. French acting version; ends immediately at the death of Beatrice-Joanna.

668 La remplacante, ed. Pierre Messaien. In Theatre anglais: Moyen age et XVIe siecle, ed. Desclee, De Brouwer. Paris, 1946. Pp. 1181-1237. (**Gallenca)

Part Five: Bibliographies

(Short forms of titles used in references in Part Four of the bibliography and elsewhere for unviewed items are given in parentheses following the full entry.)

669 Logan, Terence P. and Denzell S. Smith, eds. The New Intellectuals: A Survey and Bibliography of Recent Studies in English Renaissance Drama. Lincoln: University of Nebraska Press, 1977. Contains a section on "Cyril Tourneur," ed. Charles R. Forker, pp. 248-80, which includes a review of the Revenger's Tragedy authorship controversy in the "Canon" discussion, p. 268-71.

670 ----------. The Popular School: A Survey and Bibliography of Recent Studies in English Renaissance Drama. Lincoln: Universitiy of Nebraska Press, 1975. A selective, primarily modern bibiography and bibliographic notes are provided on each of the major figures of the period. The Middleton listing is by John B. Brooks, pp. 50-84; it is partially annotated and contains an extensive listing of textual studies that discusses the dating of each play, a list of general sources, and specific items on each play. (Popular School)

670a Brooks, John B. "Recent Studies in Middleton." English Literary Renaissance 14 (1984): 114-128. Provides an update to the Middleton bibliography as far as 1981. (Popular School Update)

671 The Modern Humanities Research Association Annual Bibliography of English Language and Literature. Published annually, covering material up to three years previous. Covers Middleton under "Seventeenth Century." Complements the MLA Bibliography (see 672); more detailed on review articles, monographs, and dissertations, but not published as quickly. (MHRA Bibliography)

672 The Modern Language Association of America International Bibliography. Published annually, with the contents covering up to the previous two years. Annotated since the 1983 edition. The most comprehensive bibliograpy in the modern languages; covers Middleton under "English Literature, Seventeenth Century." (MLA Bibliography)

673 Penninger, Frieda Elaine, ed. English Drama to 1660 (Excluding Shakespeare): A Guide to Literary Sources. Detroit: Gale Research Company, 1976. A brief guide to major sources; Middleton is discussed on pp. 309-311.

674 "Recent Literature of the English Renaissance." In Studies in English Literature (SEL); published annually in the Spring issue. A helpful, discursive, annual update; lengthy reviews of major monographs and collections, with occasional discussions of articles and of trends in criticism.

675 Ribner, Irving, compiler. Tudor and Stuart Drama. New York: Appleton-Century-Crofts, 1966. A Goldentree Bibliography, with useful items both in the section on Thomas Middleton (pp. 46-47) and in the sections on general critical and historical studies.

676 ----------, with Clifford C. Huffman. Tudor and Stuart Drama, Second Edition. 1978. Updated entries.

677 Tannenbaum, Samuel A. and Dorothy R., compilers. "Thomas Middleton." Elizabethan Bibliographies. Port Washington, New York: Kennikat Press, 1967. Vol. V, second of four articles, each paginated separately. First published 1940.

678a Donovan, Dennis, G., compiler. "Thomas Middleton 1939-1965." Elizabethan Bibliographies Supplement 1. London: Nether Press, 1967. Pp. 15-36. Together with Tannenbaum's listings, these make up the standard bibliography of Middleton's work, with the additional update in The Popular School (see 670).

679 Tucker, Kenneth. A Bibliography of Writings by and about John Ford and Cyril Tourneur. Boston: G.K. Hall, 1977. Contains an index on The Revenger's Tragedy authorship controversy, listing authors for Middleton and for Tourneur and those apparently neutral, with references to his full Tourneur bibliography.

680 Watson, George, ed. The New Cambridge Bibliography of English Literature. Cambridge: Cambridge University Press, 1974. The Middleton listing is in Volume 1 (600-1660), columns 1646 to 1654. A reasonably comprehensive listing of the major items, including both articles and monographs. The Middleton article is greatly expanded in this edition, reflecting the increased interest in his work in the last thirty years. (New Cambridge Bibliography)

681 Wells, Stanley, ed. _English Drama (Excluding Shakespeare)_. London: Oxford University Press, 1975 (the Select Bibliographical Guides). "Thomas Middleton" (pp. 76-86 [essay] and 94-97 [listings]) is edited by Samuel Schoenbaum, and includes major nineteenth-century and twentieth-century criticism as far as the early seventies, with the major items discussed in an essay that traces changes in Middleton's literary profile. (_English Drama_)

APPENDIX: THE CANON OF THOMAS MIDDLETON'S PLAYS

The following plays have been attributed, in whole or in part, to Middleton. They are listed in alphabetical order, with suggestions about dating and authorship (from *Annals*, ed. Harbage and Schoenbaum, from Bald, "Chronology", and from Lake, *Canon*; see 046, 167 and 147) in parentheses following.

Anything for a Quiet Life	(+ Webster; c. 1621)
The Bloody Banquet	(?Drue; pub. 1639)
Blurt, Master Constable	(+ Dekker; 1601-2)
The Changeling	(+ Rowley; 1622)
A Chaste Maid in Cheapside	(1613)
A Fair Quarrell	(+ Rowley; 1615-16)
The Family of Love	(+ Dekker? or Barry?; 1602 or 1606-7)
A Game at Chess	(1624)
Hengist, King of Kent, or The Mayor of Queenborough	(1615-20)
The Honest Whore, Part I	(+ Dekker; 1604)
Macbeth, III.v	(+ Shakespeare; 1606-11)
A Mad World, My Masters	(1604-7)
A Match at Midnight	(?Rowley; 1621-3)
Michaelmas Term	(1604)
More Dissemblers Besides Women	(c. 1615)
The Nice Valour	(+ Fletcher?; 16cc)
No Wit, No Help Like a Woman's	(c. 1615)
The Old Law	(+ Rowley and Massinger?; c. 1616)
The Phoenix	(1602)
The Puritan	( )
The Revenger's Tragedy	(1608)
The Roaring Girl	(+ Dekker; 1607-8)
The Second Maiden's Tragedy	(1611)
The Spanish Gipsy	(+ Rowley? or Dekker or Ford? 1623)
Timon of Athens (I.ii and III)	(+ Shakespeare; 1602)
A Trick to Catch the Old One	(c. 1606)
The Widow	(1616)

INDEX OF PLAYS

References are to item numbers; underlined references are to editions. The collected editions of Bullen (item 578) and Dyce (579) are not included in these individual listings. An index of items discussing non-dramatic works follows the play index.

NON-DRAMATIC WORKS